AF243905

BY EMILIE GLEN

The Writings of Emilie Glen 1: Poems from Chapbooks

The Writings of Emilie Glen 2: Fiction and Prose Poems

The Writings of Emilie Glen 3: Poems from Magazines

The Writings of Emilie Glen 4: Poems from Manuscripts

THE WRITINGS OF EMILIE GLEN

4

POEMS FROM MANUSCRIPTS

Selected and edited by Brett Rutherford

THE POET'S PRESS
Pittsburgh, PA

www.poetspress.org

ISBN 0-922558-87-6
This is the 228th publication of The Poet's Press
Also published in Adobe Acrobat (PDF) format.

Cover art:
Wood engraving
by John DePol

THE POET'S PRESS
2209 Murray Avenue #3
Pittsburgh, PA 15217

TABLE OF CONTENTS

POEMS FROM 77 COLUMBIA STREET (1960s-1979)

MORE POEMS FROM MAGAZINES

ABOUT EMILIE GLEN

Meeting Emilie

It was my first Greenwich Village poetry reading. One rainy night in the muggy summer of 1969, I ascended the subway stairs from the Christopher Street station for the first time. Like most very, very young poets I carried a heavy ledger book full of most of my poems, a yellow legal pad, and my hand-bound first chapbook. Using the poetry listings in *The Village Voice*, and the requisite beginner's street map to Manhattan, I walked several blocks east to the Waverly Theater. I was getting close: the right street, almost the right address. Ah, there it was, on a dark metal door: a hand-lettered sign pointing me in and up. In the dimly-lit loft above, I joined a circle of anxious poets, shuffling their papers and waiting their turn to read. They all seemed to know one another, and they were a motley crew, from hippies to aging Beats, from brawny blue-collar types to wispy graybeards.

At the center of the circle, the poet Emilie Glen presided. She was a tall woman, perhaps in her early fifties (so little did I suspect!) with striking red hair, dressed in an odd assortment of clothes, a cross between Baby Jane Hudson and Lolita. Her voice was refined, every syllable crisp and clear, her poems lithe little narratives of New York life, spiced with delicious word play. She read her poetry with us, as one of us, not as one enthroned as judge, critic, gatekeeper.

Emilie — one of the major doyens of the open poetry scene — was adept at making everyone feel welcome. Beginners, mumblers, hopeless versifiers, stray mental patients, and fine poets jostled elbow to elbow at her readings. Everyone had his or her moment in the sun, either in the open "one around" where everyone warmed up by reading just one poem, or, for those who dared, with a full five minutes of self-glorying performance. There was usually a "featured reader" who did two twenty-minute sets, and, naturally, being featured was to attain the pinnacle, your name listed in the newspapers, and your work, perhaps, noticed by some visiting publisher, agent or love-of-your-life. And even though the awful and the truly great presented themselves before her, one sensed that she knew the difference. We were all workers in the vineyard, but there was no confusing Ripple with Moët et Chandon. In the New York poetry scene, one quickly learns that bad art is accorded polite silence, while great art is embraced with an ardor that would shock New Englanders.

This was the 1960s-1970s Manhattan poetry scene. Although venues like St. Mark's in the East Village had more celebrity status with their indelible associations with the art scene and underground culture, the West Village had numerous poetry outlets, where a wide mix of styles and degrees of talent blossomed. Ree Dragonette, Emilie's arch-rival, ran a poetry-theatre salon from her loft in Westbeth. Other venues included St. John's in the Village; Poetry on the Piers at Gansevoort Pier on the Hudson; Boruk Glasgow's at his East 14th Street loft, downstairs from a boxing gym (imagine those two groups eyeing one another suspiciously on the stairs!); Risa Korsun's events at a church at St. Mark's Place and at the Baha'i Center; and the New York Poets' Cooperative at various cafes and apartments. Uptown, Marguerite Harris hosted a series at a tavern, Dr. Generosity's, although she frowned upon featuring poets who "read too frequently below 14th Street." Poets and poetry lovers in those days had their choice, on any given night, of a good half-dozen poetry events. Many of these organizations and venues came and went; Emilie Glen's readings and salons, running for more than two decades, outlasted most of them.

The vast majority of these events were listed as "featured and open," which meant that after hearing the featured poet, members of the audience were welcome to share their work. They did, and the most active poets on the scene had the chance to premiere new work, and get practice in front of live audiences, several nights a week.

Emilie welcomed me enthusiastically and we soon became friends. For the next two decades, I would see Emilie weekly, sometimes daily. She hosted poets twice a week — Sunday nights at her 77 Columbia Street high-rise apartment, and another night at various West Village lofts or theaters. In addition, we would meet at various old-fashioned restaurants: Schrafft's, Macy's Fountain, Rumpelmayers. If I cooked dinner at home, my famous honey-crumb meatloaf was mandatory, after I assured Emilie it contained "no alarming spices." Fortunately she didn't inquire about herbs.

Although she rode to her dinner engagements on a bicycle, dressed in short skirts and pink leotards, red hair flying, Emilie was not the rag-tag Village Bohemian she appeared to be. She had been a child of privilege. Taken on the Grand Tour of Europe as a young girl, she had seen Paris, the Harz Mountains, Rome. Later, her family summered at Chautauqua. She trained as a child prodigy under concert pianist Ernest Hutchison, and continued on to Juilliard School in Manhattan under his tutelage.

Unlike the rest of us, Emilie did not have to go to work on Monday. Or Tuesday. She was provided for, modestly but securely. She was able to do what we all dreamt of: to devote her life to poetry.

Emilie was married, but her husband, Charlie Dash, was absent and seldom mentioned. It was clear from Emilie's carefree ways, and her stunning indifference to financial matters, that her late father, and her indulgent husband, had left her financially independent, at least enough so to continue living in Manhattan to pursue her art full-time.

Emilie's apartment at 77 Columbia Street was in a respectable high-rise co-op, overlooking the East River. The Lower East Side neighborhood, bordering Delancey Street and the Manhattan Bridge, was quite sinister at night. Yet poets came each Sunday evening, year-round, by cab, car, or subway, in everything from jeans to fur coats. One of the most bedraggled poets, Richard Bush Brown, was repeatedly mugged on his way home from Emilie's high-rise. All of us had what we imagined to be "close calls" on those nights, but we kept coming back.

The cast of characters at Emilie's readings was fascinating. There I met the phenomenal Barbara A. Holland, and most of the other New York poets I would later publish, including Donald Lev, Shirley Powell, Boria Sax, Joel Zeltzer, Claudia Dobkins-Dikinis, Boruk Glasgow, and John Burnett Payne.

The sad-sack poet-playwright Richard Davidson was omnipresent, always mooching a sandwich ("Could you spare a slice of bread? Oh, thank you. Some mustard on that would be nice. Would you happen to have a slice of cheese I could put on that? Ah. I see you have some leftover ham there. Could I put a little of that on my bread?...") Davidson and Glen shared a passion for the theater and she frequently accompanied him to plays. He got free tickets to many off-off Broadway productions in his capacity as drama reviewer for the *Daily World* (a Socialist newspaper which ironically never paid him a penny for his journalism). I would later direct and publish Davidson's verse play, *Song of Walt Whitman*.

Charlie Gould, a paper merchant's messenger with an unnerving resemblance to Joseph Stalin, doted on Emilie. He gifted her with a handsome pastel he had done, copying one of Doré's engravings from Dante's *Il Paradiso*. Gould broke with Emilie in fury after she depicted him in a poem, "To Let," revealing that he had taken in a teen runaway girl. He would later go off to live with the Hare Krishnas in West Virginia and came to believe that he had discovered the Ur-Language.

Gustav Davidson, an expert on the mythos of angels, and various officers of the Poetry Society of America, were often there, too, for Emilie was a longtime member of that august group. The PSA, with its headquarters at Gramercy Park, was the domain of effete versifiers and poetic dowagers. Emilie dragged me, squirming, to a couple of its meetings; as I was still in my rebellious Whitman-Ginsberg period, it was excruciating. She was obliged to admit it was rather unseemly that the officers kept awarding themselves the group's monthly poetry prize. She resigned from the Poetry Society later when they opened their membership to anyone willing to pay dues. In her day, members had to be recommended, and pass muster with writing samples. Considering the sclerotic sonnetizing I heard at the PSA, Emilie must have been regarded there as a wild, modernist.

Perhaps attending Emilie's readings was the closest some of these elder poets ever came to a den of Beatniks.

Poets, translators, scholars, students, and just plain lovers of poetry flocked to Emilie's salon, dominated by her fine baby grand piano. Some nights she would play her staples, her favorite being the Funeral March from Beethoven's A-Flat Piano Sonata. When I purchased my first harpsichord and gravitated away from the piano, Emilie was aghast. Bach and Scarlatti and Handel were fine and good, but how could you play Liszt on an instrument with no pedals? Fortunately for our musical accord, I remained just as devoted to the Romantics as to the Baroque. But when Emilie came to my loft, she looked at my two-manual harpsichord rather as one would a basket full of cobras.

When Emilie's folk-singing daughter Glenda married and gave birth to a child, the sudden death of the son-in-law (both alcoholic and epileptic), induced Emilie to make a drastic change in her living conditions: in 1979, she gave up the Columbia Street co-op, and sold her piano, to move into the brownstone tenement building at 77 Barrow Street to help her daughter care for her infant son, John. One poem in the present volume (Volume 3) refers to a prior move from Emilie's original brownstone apartment on West 15th Street, where she had her grand piano.

Emilie took the apartment adjacent to Glenda's. It was dark, narrow, only two rooms. The toilet was in the hall. Emilie slept on a narrow bed next to the kitchen, and turned the living room into the best semblance she could of her old parlor. The Sunday night readings resumed. The terrifying night walk down Delancey Street was replaced by the welcoming streets of Cherry Lane and Barrow Street. Walking up five flights of stairs was a small price to pay for the poetic thrills that awaited one. The Village location also meant that poets could repair to a local coffeehouse after the reading was over, for more poetry talk and gossip. Such nights often went on until the cafes closed (the Bohemia we have now lost forever in the Yuppie-infested decades since).

In giving up her piano, Emilie had made the final break with her first Muse. She had trained as a concert pianist, and so long as there was a piano in the house, she was never really severed from that early promise. Now she would only play, with faltering memory, when she came upon a piano in a café or in someone's home. The piano would now become a ghost, its notes sounding but never dying in her later poems. I never heard Emilie complain about the appalling condition of her apartment, with its bathtub in the kitchen and decrepit stove and refrigerator: only the loss of the piano seemed to diminish her spirit.

Her Life: A Choice Among Muses

Emilie Carolyn Glen was older — by decades — than she wanted us to believe. When interviewed, she would terminate the conversation when the delicate question of age came up. In the 1977 *International Who's Who in Poetry*, Emilie listed her birth date as 1927. In a later directory, she revised that to read 1937[1]. Actually, Emilie was born around 1906, making her 63 years old when I first met her in 1969. Her birthday was March 13.

Early in her career, she worked for Macmillan Publishing Company and did a stint with Fairchild Publications — from what I can gather, as a reporter for *Women's Wear Daily*. In a poet biographical note in 1947, she indicates that she "covered fashion shows, visited wholesale houses, and saw child models at work.[2]" In this note, she says that her daughter Glenda was then seven years old.

Her university experience included a full course at Syracuse University. The sorority Alpha Phi Alpha lists her in the graduating class of 1928. Emilie continued to Columbia University and went on with her music studies with Ernest Hutchison at the Juilliard School.

At some point, literature took precedence over music. Emilie was not clear in her own mind why her career as a pianist ended, but the competitiveness and misogyny of the classical music field may have contributed. There were then only a handful of women among the premiere artists of the keyboard, and virtually no women in orchestras. In the literary world women, while embattled, could at least expect a modicum of success.

I suspect Emilie also realized that the choice between being a creative artist and a performing artist was one that had to be made. Many people could play Beethoven and Liszt; only Emilie could write Emilie's poems.

During the 1940s, Emilie worked on the staff of *The New Yorker*. Only a single, brief notice, in 1942[3], credits her as a writer there, however. She may have worked for the publisher as a behind-the-scenes fact-checker. Emilie related to me how *The New Yorker* checked every reference in every piece they published, even in poems. She recalled that a number of women hired by the magazine in the 1940s were let go at war's end when "the men came home."

---

[1] Emilie was listed in *Who's Who in U.S. Writers, Editors and Poets*, 2nd edition 1988, and in successive editions through 1995-96. Her birth date there was listed as 1937! She was also listed in *Who's Who of American Women*, 2nd edition, 1961-62 and 1964-65. I would be grateful to receive photocopies or transcripts of these listings.

[2] *Epoch*, Cornell University, 1947.

[3] Russell Maloney, "Comment", *The New Yorker*, October 24, 1942, p. 11

Editing a Manhattan-based Congregational Church magazine appears to be Emilie's last paying job. Several sample copies were among Emilie's surviving papers.

During the 1940s, Emilie wrote as much prose as poetry, and had her stories published in *The Prairie Schooner* and H.L. Mencken's *American Mercury*. One story chosen by Mencken went on to be included in *Best American Short Stories*. The fiction that I have been able to locate is included in the second volume of this series.

The Coffeehouse Years

In the 1960s, the poet found herself a fixture in several Greenwich Village coffeehouses, where she read her poems and played piano. In response to requests from patrons at the coffeehouses, starting in 1966, Emilie had little mimeographed chapbooks of her current poems run off and hand-stapled (*Coffeehouse Poems, Mad Hatter, Paint and Turpentine*, and others). All but one of the poet's published chapbooks, including those done later by The Poet's Press, are in Volume 1 of this series.

Emilie performed in children's theater, most notably playing the Witch in productions of Hansel and Gretel. Stage-struck, she could not resist joining a small theater company on West 14th Street called Dramatis Personae, when they also offered her a Sunday afternoon poetry venue in their theater. Steven Baker, the director, had landed on the gimmick of staging plays with massive nudity, the audience members invited to shed their own clothes, dressed in just-legal "flimsies" as they watched over-endowed actors and actresses simulate Roman orgies, the sins of Sodom, Witches' Sabbaths and other sexual *tableaux vivants*. Emilie was the only clothed member of the cast, portraying priestesses, witches, or nuns.

The stint with Dramatis Personae ended when Baker decided that plays for gay audiences were more lucrative. He fired all the actresses and successive productions were revues titled simply *Boys, Boys, Boys*. The theater later acquired a reputation for after-hours drinking and drugs.

Once Emilie was established at the Barrow Street address, she was able to attract a large and diverse group of poets and listeners to her weekly or twice-weekly salons (Sundays and Tuesdays). If she found a loft, atelier or theater space willing to host her, the Sunday events shifted to the other venue.

Listed in *The Village Voice* and partially funded by grant money, Emilie attracted a big crowd and was able to pay her featured poets. The mix was eclectic, and one could hear a stodgy college professor followed by a longshoreman. She fed everyone with juices and snacks, which the modest pass-the-hat donations scarcely covered.

Emilie was an avid birder (or bird-watcher, to use the term she knew) and for many years haunted Central Park with binoculars, a member of that elite society of The Rambles. A number of poems in this volume spring from her observations of birds, and those who observe and document them.

Her love for cats seemed to her non-contradictory, so long as the cats stayed indoors, the birds safely out. There were always cats in Emilie's apartment, an amalgam of hers and those left behind by her daughter. Hundreds of poems from her pen on animal topics found their way into print. Poems about birds and cats are, admittedly, rather easy to place, but Glen's best animal poems rise above the crowd of bourgeois robins and mewling kittens.

Although Emilie had not traveled abroad since childhood, she, like Thoreau, traveled much where she lived. Emilie's bicycle was spotted in all boroughs, and she would even venture by subway and bicycle to Far Rockaway. She was a year-round swimmer, and swam with the Polar Bears Club. Her stamina was incredible, as was her resistance to doctors and medicine. Once, crossing a Village Street, Emilie and I were both thrown to the ground by a sudden and terrific wind. She picked herself up and resumed the walk as though nothing had happened. For days she sported an alarming lump on her forehead, but nothing would persuade her to visit a doctor or emergency room. I would have suspected her of a Christian Science upbringing, but I never heard a conventionally religious word from her. We both shared a gagging disdain for poets who came to her readings with little hymns and mini-sermons.

Some stories in Volume 2 suggest a Caribbean sojourn in the early 1960s, an uncharacteristic vacation, but then, the sea was always Emilie's first love. She captures local atmosphere in "Ciudad" and gives us several portraits of strong Caribbean women, making us wish that she had traveled more.

★　★　★　★　★

My move to Providence ended my almost weekly meetings with Emilie. I brought her to Providence once to do a reading at the series I ran at my house on Transit Street. She came with her grandson and one of his schoolmates. We had a splendid visit and Emilie charmed everyone with her reading; but it was evident that dementia was taking its toll. Friends in New York began taking an active interest in her welfare, most notably poet Vivanna Grell. Others who became aware that Emilie's finances had run out sent "care packages" of food. The poetry readings became chaotic as Emilie lost control of her scheduling, and sometimes two or even three poets would show up, each thinking him- or herself the featured reader.

Thanks to the inept management of her finances by her bankers, what had been a secure income from interest was turned into a charge account which Emilie and her grandson quickly exhausted: every time she ran up the credit card to the limit, her financial "advisor" sold off more stock.

Finally, Emilie was left nearly destitute, and as dementia set in, she could no longer find her way even a few blocks from her house without becoming hopelessly lost. Diagnosed with advanced Alzheimer's, she was committed to a nursing home. There, she gradually lost all interest in poetry, and in a final act of will, stopped taking food. She died on December 30, 1995.

The Emilie Glen I prefer to remember — Emilie as she was from the 1940s through the 1980s — was the poet's poet. Every writer who knew her stood in awe of her ability to work day after day, year after year, seemingly without a "block." Rejections that would throw other writers into a depression just rolled off her. She typed and mailed out a dozen or more poems every day. Each day's mail contained rejection slips, acceptances, tear sheets, printed magazines with her poems in them, and, once in a great while, a tiny check. On and on and on, for four decades she had done this, untiring, unremitting.

Working this hard, Emilie saw literally thousands of her poems published. Until the sorrows of her family life overcame her, she had the privilege of being a full-time poet. She kept herself free of romantic entanglements, her mind free from cant and religion, and never touched alcohol or drugs. She knew exactly what the Muse required, and Nature had endowed her with prodigious health.

As a New York personality and friend of poets, Emilie Glen was one of the happiest lights of Greenwich Village in what we now know to be its literary Indian Summer.

I miss Emilie, my first friend in New York, and the first poet to welcome me to the larger community of poets.

—Brett Rutherford
Pittsburgh, December 2015

(A longer version of this essay appears in Volume 1, with more biographical information about the poet, and more details about her published books and chapbooks)

FOREWORD TO VOLUME 4

The present volume was constructed from a shopping bag full of typed manuscripts, the last part of the Emilie Glen papers passed to me a few years after her death. Some were typewritten originals, some faint carbon copies, and a handful turned out to be, on close inspection, pages from printed small press magazines or chapbooks. None of the papers were duplicates of the tear-sheet collection published as Volume 3 in this series, so the poems presented here are assumed to be either abandoned sketches, or copies of poems that may have been submitted or even accepted in magazines. Since so many small press and international journals are not indexed anywhere, there may be many hundreds or even thousands of published poems that will turn up over time. So it is only a provisional assumption that almost none of these poems had seen print.

Since Emilie and I culled her poems for the chapbooks and books we produced together, and since the tear-sheet collection was mined for Volume 2 of this series, it might be assumed that the present volume is "bottom drawer" material. In fact, I passed on about 10% of the poems in the manuscript collection, accepting all the rest as either promising lyric sketches/fragments, or as finished poems as good as anything else the poet had done. Most are much shorter than the works already in this series, but that could also reflect my editorial bias toward narrative and longer poems. Emilie was just as adept at the one-off, snapshot poem.

What I wrote about the tear-sheet collection could just as well describe the 172 poems gathered here: "The Emilie we know from the first volume is still here in spades: poet, actress, pianist, bird-watcher, cat-lover, nature rhapsodist, the woman of Manhattan with a piercing eye for character and image. She *is* the city, the street, the windows, the bridges and tunnels, the parks and fountains, the desperate dreamers on the doorsteps."

There are a few surprises. Tough and blunt as Emilie was about life and human behavior, her language was usually restrained and formal, in keeping with a literary woman born in 1906. Her immersion in the off-off-Broadway world in the 1970s, however, brought her in contact with a theater company that produced sexually-charged plays with nudity, in which she was frequently cast in the only clothed role — nun, priestess, or narrator. This world bled into her poetry salon, and poets with racy content appeared amid Emilie's Poetry Society of America friends. One gentleman who attended the theater productions, where the audience also undressed and put on translucent "flimsies," insisted on reading at her salon so attired. It was not pretty. Emilie's revolt against the language she was hearing came out in her short poem, "Poem Porn." (Her other poems about the nudie theater are collected in Volume 1.)

The poems from her Greenwich Village years that are personal, depict tenement life from the vantage of her fifth-floor walkup (bathroom in the hall), where she moved to be near her troubled, alcoholic daughter, and where she raised her grandson as a single parent. She finds beauty amid the fire escapes and limited vistas, writes sadly about the death of her daughter, and celebrates trips to Coney Island with her grandson. The poem, "Fridge Saga," was a delight to hear, and proof that she bore her tenement burden with good cheer.

The poems from Columbia Street on the Lower East Side pre-date the move to the West Village, and see New York from the rooftops. There, she still had her piano, and ventured forth to play in cafés. Emilie had related to me, in horror, the time she spent working at one coffee house run by a flamenco player. In 1967, she published a poem, "Shadowed Corner" (see Volume 2), about the owner being stalked by a death vendetta. Among Emilie's papers I found a longer poem, describing the women in the café, so terrified of the crazed owner that they are considering poisoning him. It is one of the most intense and personal of all her poems, clearly written in present-tense terror. On inspection of the manuscript, I discovered that it was copied from a mimeographed page, much like one of her early hand-made chapbooks. It is possible that Emilie published this and withdrew it, as it does not appear in any of the chapbooks gathered in Volume 1. She might have withdrawn the work under threat. The poem sees day again here, with its original title, "Register His Hands, He's A Killer."

While most poets write much, maybe too much, about the literary life, Emilie seldom does so. She doesn't gossip about other poets. She doesn't peddle manifestos. And she doesn't complain about rejections and the dismal return on investment of the poetic life. One atypical, wry poem, "Crack Our Code," makes fun of bizarre poetry journal titles.

The most surprising poem in the book, to me, is "Middle Of," an experiment in stream-of-consciousness.

The book could be read as a journal or scrapbook of its time and place, and Glen does not shy away from recounting lurid crimes, such as a murder inside the Metropolitan Opera House. She recoils from environmental catastrophes such as Three Mile Island and the madness of wars and politics, but she is not inherently a social poet. She is aloof, an ashcan painter among poets. In the last years, her poems of personal loss nearly overwhelmed her journalistic instinct, but I think the eternal child still emerges under it all.

— Brett Rutherford
Pittsburgh, PA, March 2017

POEMS FROM 77 BARROW STREET
1979-1990

Panchito's
MEXICAN RESTAURANT

BLOOD ON THE

Take back that dollar bill
    there's blood on it —

Blood on the moon, maybe,
    but not on the bill.
Could be cherry soda   cough medicine

Come   take it back.
I've seen blood   I know blood
The police come to me to locate bodies
    which I can do sometimes to the very swamp
        the very clump of black-eyed susans
Someone bled to death on that bill

LITTER

Poets   poets
        everywhere poets
My apartment chaired with poets
Poets on the window ledge
    none out the window as yet
Poets in the bathroom
    at loose or constipated scribbling
Poem in the pot tonight:
guess I'll pour in a pint of water
    and bring it to a boil.

BLOOD RED

Gentle gardener
        gentle as your flower petals
lilies beaten down by rain-wind
        you tie tenderly to a touch of wood
        coddle your rose bushes through the winter
        renew the soil
Gentle gardener
        not   so gentle
All but flowers your enemy
you shoot bunnies   raccoons   woodchucks
        mash all crawlers
        in the name of your flowerheads
could kill anyone who tramples

It is said in the village
        that you killed a motorist
        caught pulling up your forget-me-nots
            by the roots
If there is a body under the compost heap
        nobody investigates
Gentle gardener
        it so happens most of your flowers
            are blood red.

FRIDGE SAGA

Mount Everest on the fifth floor
     of our brownstone

With a forlorn glance at the snow-blinding refrigerator
       somneone has left in the hallway,
    I turn the key to my rust-streaked relic
      crowded with distracting stick-ons
    the freezer door balking
    remaining shelves tilting at the least weight
      light switch broken
could kick my abominable fridge

Out there the mountain of snows
     a virgin ice-box   whose?
Crowding by it
my Portuguese neighbor tells me in sign language
that the splendid one is too large
   for his kitchen space
He wants me to give it a home
   throws his arms about my neck
when I clap hands in joyous acceptance

The far-near grail mine   almost
My Portuguese neighbor and his friend
cart my slum-box into the hall
    rain   sweat on the white marvel
    pant   grunt   thud to a stop
His fellow worker tells me in somewhat English
   they must remove the already-shaky door
   to my apartment
Edging the stove down a few inches
they angle the great one into place
while I figure out how I can shrink past,
   eliminate my more corpulent guests,

Mountain of snows
We embrace under its splendor
I explore a labyrinth of shelves
    door tray shaped for each individual egg
deep freeze illumined   unending ice cubes
    Soon my disgrace out in the hall
    will be down and out.
The foods that crowded my old box
    are puppies in a huge cave.
I tune in   turn on   to super cool

Now I do the sweating
    when the motor grundges to a halt
    not even responding to my smart slap
    as to a new-born babe
I phone my mechanic friend
    who pronounces the mighty one dead

I call in my neighbor
who claps his hands to his head
    His friend explains
for being inherited from someone else
    it worked pretty well
    considering it was moved around too much

My fridge   my fridge
    my working fridge
    gone from the upper hall
We race down the stairs and out into the street
    by the garbage cans
There it is humiliated by the probing sun
    heavy as the cross
my fridge being sweated back up the stairs again
    by the panting men

My fridge in its rightful place
    I pat it   stroke its eczema
    open the door tenderly
finger the blisters I once tried to pop

    smile when the tray tilts
    listen to the hum of a working fridge
enjoy the stick-ons
    Han and Luke and little E.T.
    the Ewoks   the Gremlins
    Pac Man   Snoopy
Who sees the rust for the stick-ons?
    I kiss   yes kiss   my fridge

PAPER CUTS

Does Dracula bother you?
    Sky Lab?   DC-10s?
My carnivorous monster
devours me daily at my desk
    devours   regurgitates   devours
Paper   paper   paper   paper
    I live in a paperwork cloister
    offer prayers to paper
    am becoming a paper ghost
Nameless   faceless
    my daymare monster
    gives me nightmares
leaves just enough blood
    to sustain me at my paperwork
From out my paper cuts
    I bleed only ink.

BREATH INSTANT

     His space rocket
     His tree of lights —
The Empire State Building.
     He vows by his invalid window
he will catch the breath-instant
     when the tower lights darken.
Always misses,
     looks away   distracted.
Night of his death
     limned in the window
     across his features
          the going out

NO NOISE

My watch
               rushes
makes no
               but rushes
makes no noise
               but rushes
                         me.

GREATEST RAGE

In-staring
     You press your fingers
        To the lips of silence,
You alone
     In a living room at the sport
Of relating
     Their moment of greatest rage.
Is your rage a dragon
     You're afraid to let off the leash?
One tells how be beat up his school principal
     And was sent off to the CCC's,
Another tells of ripping the table-cloth
     Out from under the dishes
When two talked across him
     As if he weren't there,
Another of breaking the piano chair,
     Tearing up his music
When the A Major Polonaise
     Wouldn't leap to his fingers.
You   you alone
        In-stare

SCAREDY CAT

My little boy
       is my Big Brother.
How can that be?
Just five years old,
he has me circusing
       in a fright
climbing   jumping   walking on stilts
       sliding down poles.
Must have jogging shoes
       to keep from twisting
       my spindly ankles
while keeping up with my big brother son.

Scaredy cat   again the hoot of *scaredy cat*
Come on   again   *Come on, you can do it.*

An honor that my big brother   my small son
      wants cowardly-lion me
      in his games.
Always tagged after   never tagging
      Come on   come on
as he streaks up mesh fences.
But my feet are too large
      used to be too small
too short   too tall
      my big brother son
      beckoning me toward broken bones

POOR

Poor
      we all talk poor
                  poor
Rich
      the earth is richly growing
        corn two-leafing
      fields ready for wheat
      muck lands rich in celery
        herbs greening
        cows grazing
Poor
        talking poor
          lilies fragrant past Chanel
Poor
        while the earth bursts its bracts
Poor
        in valleys of abundance

OUTDANCED

New moon
          up sky fields
pales by UNION DIME in towered neons
          Odile dancing
          Odette ghosting

TRASH

Manhattan trash
  tempts us to rag-pick
Designers of stage sets
  find the stuff of chimeras
Sculptors collect machine-age materials.
Collage artists roll in asphodel.
My friend rehabilitates his apartment
 with trash he rehabilitates
such as apothecary drawers he hand rubs
 to the mellow shine of oak

Midtown trash another turf
  reams of paper
  stacks of manila envelopes
  swivel chairs from bankrupt firms
fabrics in the garment district
  scraps of fur scraps of leather.
Our streets may not be paved with gold
  but our trash will do
East Sixties for old wardrobes
More modest neighborhoods toss out too
  No particle of likely trash
   is ever lost
  only transmuted

TEACHER

Comet teacher
         Titan teacher
Can it be you on the bus
         nineteen years later?
Look my way,
Recognize me that I may recognize you.
Didn't you go off to Stillwater Oklahoma,
      Manhattan years ago?
Dynamo you beside the still waters,
Sidney T.   Sidney T. Gresham,
Teacher of creative writing,
Creative teacher of writing.
      Yes   you taught me the craft of fiction
      but it was the Yes of you
        that taught me.

Turn   look   Sidney T.
      Is it you?   I must know,
Little man thinking tall for us,
Slit little eyes almost set in your slender nose
      with its unexpected upturn,
      stubby fingers electric charged.
Looked forward to your evening classes
      as to a first-night play,
      house lights dimming
      curtain going up.
An almost-deserted building in midtown,
      cooing of doves
      on some inner ledge.
Are you or are you not my flame teacher?
Turn, why don't you?   See me:

Sidney T. Gresham saying   *Write*   *Write*   *Write*
      as I imploded
      toward the great explosion,
Saying *If you keep on like this*
You'll be a great writer by the time you're forty.

Three years to go.
Your one eye more of a slit than I remember —
Why, you've no eye at all.
            It's been gouged out.
                Can't be you, can it?
You have the third   the pineal eye.
Shine its light on me,
            almost the forties of your prediction,
                and I am nowhere:
editor of a trade paper,
            a wife and two boys.
Only a spare-time writer,
            winner of one small prize,
printed in one anthology,
            a few little magazines.
You are turning   glancing
            but you don't light to me

Bus nineteen years later,
Perhaps we both know better than to speak.
Someone slips into the seat beside me.
            I turn back to see you
            looking at me in depth.
Why you moved forward   to be near the door
            you're getting off the bus.
Wait   I must know,
            Were you   are you
            Sidney   Sidney T. Gresham.
In the beginning was
            In my beginning
walking along the corridor of cooing doves.
            Don't   don't leave the bus,
            Don't leave me alone
            into my forties.

COLD   COLD

Winter sharks into Indian summer
my fingers are freezing stiff
         must buy wool gloves
                 to wear   wear
         can't stop these tear explosions
I would ask my love to rub my hands warm
         the way he always

Died beside me in the night
         wool gloves to wear to his burial
hands gray with cold
         but not as cold as his   this day

WHEELS

On wheels   it comes
On wheels it goes
The street fair
    to Mulberry Street
    Feast of San Gennaro
Here   there   a neighborhood stand
    the astro ride arrives
    by tractor-trailer

Bones of some
store the memory cores
         of old-country festivals
Tarantellas danced in the streets
Same smell of sausages sweet and hot
     kettles bubbling zeppoles
The Saint is clothed in dollar bills
         gambling is by machine
You can win a puppy

VENICE IS SINKING   NEVER SINKING

Belated mermaid
Venice is sinking
     sinking into the sea
while we idle with the lost Atlantis
     sing of cathedrals rising from the waves

Venice is sinking
     sea sinking
in the weight of rotted pilings   moldering stone
Mestre shooting out profit fumes
     on church and palace
sign DANGER — FALLING ANGELS
"Save Venice" funds misappropriated   fatally delayed
     through political scraping years

One Saint in sinking Venice
     Giulia Musumeci[4]
When strong workmen ran from such wretched labor
     Giulia put her body into Venice
       her soul into Venice
Saint to Sansovino's Loggetta
     to the carvings of saints and angels,
she sweated   shivered on a scaffold
where she must crouch masked
     shooting abrasive glass beads
     to clean the pale Carrara,
       the ruddy Verona
         the Istrian stone

---

[4] Giulia Musumeci was employed by UNESCO and the Venice In Peril Fund.
Later she used lasers to clean sculptures and statues.

Improbable Venice
smiling through the sleeping beauty years
        tired Venice
        untiring Giuilia
            Saint up there
        among the saints she lives to save

TOWARD

Rivers toward
                    more than from
sea toward
                    even in the backup of rapids
the Hudson down from Lake Tear
the muddy Danube past gypsy fires
the Arno   the Vltava wherever they go
Mississippi   ghosting paddle wheels
                    in the laughter of Mark Twain
Castanet waters of the Rio Grande
Through polluted and pure,
rivers taking the earth's continents with them
Nile still in the scene   of Cleopatra's sails
Rhine of *Götterdämmerung*
Blood of the Volga
                    towards   always towards

BY WATER

Glimpsing my blue green aura
the photographer says   I see you by water
        me Pisces   by water
We walk to the river
        the once-lordly Hudson.
He poses me on the pier where I can't look out
        on the Hudson in crowns of sun.
I must smile into the black lens.
My shadow goes out on water-light
Pollution or no
        the sun will boat under   big red
The picture may catch the first ship
        to sail the river
        once pure as the mountain springs
            of its beginning

ACROSS THE HALL

Seldom look in on him
    Hear him climb the stairs
    Note his light under the door
Can cross the hall any time
    can't say I do
    busy as I am about nothing much
Comforting smell of his soup
    reminding he is in

He died in the night
    sitting at his paper-fall desk
Now that the police have sealed the door
    Oh to look in

RAIN SEEDS

Raining
            but the sky
green raining
            blue of faience
sidewalk green with rain
            Why, they're seeds!
I look up at a wall of English ivy
            rippling the red bricks
seeds enough for many ivied halls.
            Green seeds in my hair,
will I grow long green locks
            in ivy point?

DAN DE

Dan
        De
            Li
                On
Petals radiant   radiant
Discovery of Dandelion
            ripped from the earth as weeds
weeds golding the green monotony of lawns.
Dandelions rate florist shops
            street carts along with violets
            corsages
            the bride's bouquet
I kneel
            kneel to the dandelion

FRONTISPIECE

Mermaid frontispiece
        For my undersea poems
            Seapuzzles me
Cryptic little dame
        Some believe she is smug
        Others that she is insecure
One moonpulling night
        She crept off the page
I caught her green-slithering back up
        Just before the alarm went off
Smoothing her tide-tangled hair
        Adjusting her tail to the page

SIGNS

The owl and seagull
        My life signs

The owl hung all-feathered wise
above my father's roll-top desk,
        Father wise beneath the golden eyes,
ATTORNEY-AT-LAW gold-lettered
        across the long windows

Father gone
        I run around after a do-it-yourself divorce.
Failing
        I find you
        above your semi-circled desk,
A seagull is winging against the wind.
        You are my brother
        who never grew up to be a lawyer

Father   Brother
        Owl and seagull.

LIVING ROOM

People of the living room
        Here to socialize
      Sit around in plexiglass
        So separate
They view one another
        Through smoked mirrors
The cat romping round the circle
    Where everyone sits as in corners
Is reached out to
        Petted
Not so much as the touching of fingertips
    Their words are streamers
        Mostly grey
    Shooting past each other
As the cat purrs to their touch
    They ghost come
        Ghost go
    Dipping fingers
Into the warm fur of the cat
Later try to recall faces
    In the circle of corners
Remember the feel of fur

CEMENT ODE

Polka dots big as bubbles
    Bubble dots
Blue   red   orange   green
About the big white bellies
    Of cement trucks
    Circusing down the street
Two   three   four   five
    Laughing clowns
    of the construction show
See how they arrive across the way
    Like beasts to a watering hole

Bubble dots   but are they functional?
    Yes   to the joy of eyes
Spinning their fat bellies to fun dots
    Trucks of glee
Glee city spinning
    Bubble dots hosed to a glisten
    By their keepers
Dancing-dot bellies
    to a joyous shitting of cement

SCREEN TEST

Great grey elephant of the city night,
Motion picture building for underground movies,
After a foot-burn day of making the rounds,
I come into the belly of the elephant,
Come with a friend who is picking up his equipment.

We climb clanging iron landings.
Not so much as a rubber bone of a role.
Look in on the leavings
        milk cartons   spilled powder
        a rash of fragrance over old boards
        dust playing leap-mouse in the draft

through broken windows.
A torn costume hangs dirty orange
        over the pipes,
            ripped mask on a peg,
        mashed lipstick.
We surprise soft-drink bottles
        into forsaken rollings.

As to a saddle
I hoist myself to an empty stage,
before a ragged backdrop
        go into surreal lines
        from my last bit part.
Rick rummages out a small movie camera.
        But Rick   I'm not ready —
You've been ready since your birth —

With a fire bucket and a stick
I churn butter à la Marie Antoinette,
        mime the terrors of revolution —
Hold that pose for a close-up —
No, I can't stop while I'm Marie.
        Follow me with the camera.
This will be my screen test   my moon shot.
Stage   screen   I'll be wearing them for earrings

Marie Antoinette leaving me as a ghost its medium,
I sink crying to a stage
        dirtier than a chicken roost.
How were you discovered? the newsmen will query,
        and my smile will out Mona Lisa,
as I answer   In the belly of the great grey elephant.

When will the film be ready, Rick?
I was great   I know I was great.
It will be my showcase to fame.
    Why, there's no film in the camera —
        it is empty as this place.
Thought you knew it was all in fun.

NOT FOR BATHSHEBA

Bathsheba's bath
        may have splashed history
Still for me   it is my bath overwhelms
bath in an up-country house
        where the window is within touching distance
            of a mountainside so steep
        its flowers and greenery
            are vertical as a frieze
yellow lilies that out-scent my bath bubbles
        spice lupines
            ferns   lacing ferns
        leaves twining   blossoms
            purple iris   pals of buttercups
        yellow butterflies big as warblers
            singing of the robin
            mimicking thrasher
        and skeins of sun
More than clean
I am flower woods purified
        lily among lilies in Eden bath

APPLE SQUARE

Apple tree square
        never saw an apple tree
apple   apple
        apple tree square
squares I've seen around the world
        Florence   Athens   Amsterdam
My square in the Minnesota of a thousand lakes
        where for want of an apple tree
        I climbed the catalpa

TREE OF HEAVEN

Ailanthus   our city tough
        our city punk
Its stink gets around
        right through car fumes and various pollutants
        backyard weed of monoxide cities
the male flower evil-smelling
        cat-squirt stench
yet I lean out the window
        and breathe in in
should I confess to rather wallowing in its musk.

Those lime-tint florets overwhelm me
        with their trumpeting scent.
In China the tree is also known
as the celestial tree   tree of heaven
        luscious fragrance I might add.
But don't go by me —
I'm also turned on by the oaty odor of horse droppings

WINDOW

Lighted window
        at the curve of a street near midtown
deep as brownstone windows are deep
        Passersby stare up through the hill
at a mother holding a child in her arms
        Yearn in to her yearning out.

MARCH ON

Scarlet fever dark-boating me
     down a red river
       far from the shore I went.
     Performance in assembly
       Barbara Fritchie
rehearsed and rehearsed
only to be sickbed indisposed
to another's saying:
Who harms a hair on yon gray head ...

Red rivers later
   I still go down into sleep
repeating, *Who harms a hair of yon gray head*
    dies like a dog
      like a dog ...

Role of Madam Elizabeth in *Look Homeward Angel*
     lost down fever river
       past clouds of untossed flowers
     the Elizabeth lines sinking into
      like a dog
    like a dog
      march on he said.

DROUGHT

Corn shriveling
Soybeans gasping
       earth hard caked
       grazing lands dust
cattle dying   Mississippi too weak for barges
        Worst drought in a hundred years.
Are the heavens in such a budget bind
        they can't afford rain in the Midwest?
Then put us on welfare
       and give us rain stamps
or we'll march on the skies

NO HANDS

No hands
     at Bellevue
        beautiful view
No hands
     down the corridors of long walking
No hands
     on the clocks
     time-stained clocks
       whatever floor you get off
No hands
     no hands on the clock

AWAY   AWHILE

Husband of twelve years
    you died beside me in the night
Two years later
    and I still think I see you
    in easy walk down the street
Reaching home I open the door
    to tell you   tell you
I pick up the phone to call your office
    we'll have lunch together
No   no, we won't   not ever
    I say *we* a lot
forgetting that you're
    because you're not
not down there in the dark

IN THE PINK

Pink ruffled bedroom
toys everywhere about
closet puffed with dresses
floored with shoes
pink ruffled room gathering sunlight

My child room should have been bare
        to prepare me for a room on an airshaft
office shuddering with factory machines
        you can guess my recurring dream

LATE MARCH

Sitting on the steps of March
I behold the sky of late afternoon
        above the waters of the Bay
Dance of the seven veils
        late March still dancing winter
veils of lavender   veils of lime
        dusty pink   old gold
veils shifting throughout
        my cold watch on the steps
many greys   many yellows   tinged lilac
        seven veils in hints of sun

TAR STAR

Cat on the tar paper roof across
        foundering —
Oh for a Tarzan rope!
        I run down five flights
        climb a fence,
arrive just in time to catch
        the black and white in my arms
At home with me and I with him
I'm making him a beaded collar of belonging
        and hammering out a copper name plate
            for   for TAR STAR.
My eyes enter into his
his eyes have already entered into mine.

MILKWEED

Milkweed feathers the sun
        suns the air
We used to be stained with milk
        shucking the ripe pods
            to feathers for our doll pillows
Pod order of the brown seed tips,
        Jenny Milkweed seed,
I blew my breath into the feathers
            seeds out   away
never knowing till now
            that the eggs of the monarch butterfly
                were pillowed in the leaves

GOLDEN MANE

My lion's mane
        how you tousled
        when we were a thing
Back from the latest ward
        I meet you on Madison Avenue
            and I'm a bald pate

But Leonard   you have the eyes of a lion
        the moonstone eyes of a lion

WILD

Bored   the horses
                    riding bored horses
                              boring
Horses meant to be wild
            free of the metal in their jaws
jerked this way and that
            by their sensitive mouths
            whipped faster   faster
Instead of being strapped to their food
            horses should be feeding
            on the wild grasses
thundering the plains

Bored   bored   bored
            horses weighted with saddles
            shut into stables
I throw myself on my bed at the Inn.
In the lowering of the moon
I'm going to run down to the stable and free them,
            free all the bored horses

HORROR OF CANNON

All night the cannon
                killing   maiming
                      our young
takes me back to the factory
            on the other side of town

Kaboom   Kaboom
            making mincemeat of sleep

ATLANTIC CITY LULLABY

Jingle   jingle
Jangle   jingle
                Casino surf
                ocean of slot machines
                flotsam of gaming tables

Out there
                the surfing sea
                surfing   surfing
In here   jingling   jangling
                clinking   clanking
                pinging   panging
Out there
                the dark forever
                 surfing white

MARK MY

Cold
        my love
                as Triton
        Neptune's moon.
Would rather be in a sink-hole of darkness
than in the light of such a moon
        wind 1,600 mph
        400 below zero.
I'm a day flower
and when I release my sun-energy
    it will be a clash of Titans.

BUZZ   BUZZ

Bee   I'm a bee
          a black and gold bee
buzzing about these pollen-full flowers,
flying their nectar to our honey factory

Of course I sting humans
for grabbing our products
    If we bees were human hulks
we would bus to Washington
    and demonstrate

SHELL I MADE

Spiral   my shell
          Without center
So cunningly constructed
          No one can get at me
Made it myself of piano keys and cosmic dust
          Leaf laminates   powdered pine needles
              Pressed sunsets
          Tektites   flamenco
              Lilac surf
          Overall finish: lake at evening
A little dizzy always spiraling
          Never a center
I'm winding when I'm unwinding
          Unwinding when I'm winding
              No center
Yet I'm spiraling best
              Inside my shell —
If I crawled out in spiral squeeze
              Shivering out
          I would be a poor thing

AMETHYST

Jewel of my secret drawer
            exquisitely faceted
            polished to perfection
small purple sun
            not set   never worn
amethyst beyond display

SPEAKING OF WEEDS

What you don't want in your garden
            that's what a weed is.
I want them all in my garden,
        all the weeds.
Two minutes in my garden
    and they will become respectable.

ROSE OF A

Know what I'm known as?
        the nose   rose of a nose
Not for looks
        but for what it smells
A good living   just smelling

Leading houses such as Elizabeth Arden
        Estee Lauder   Helene Rubinstein
depend on my nose for the creation
        of excruciating perfumes
too little of this   too much of that
        an ineffable something missing
my nose knows   my rose of a nose

BRIGHTEST ORANGE

Bus transfers   no big deal
just pieces of paper
        until the driver in courtly fashion
transfers the giving of the transfer
        into a ceremony
Inclining towards me
he holds out the paper saying
        This is a special transfer
        a very special transfer
An orange bird fluttering in my hand

CASANOVA JUNIOR

Care to meet me?
I'm my adolescent son's telephone sitter
        every minute on the minute
Garden of girls' names
        Lorna   Gia   Linda   Melinda
        Monique   Susie   Susan
        Denise   Diane   Alissa   Violeta
Message tumbling on message
        "Tell him I'm in town today."
"I'll be in the Park."
        "He's kept me waiting on a street corner
            for more than an hour."
"It's Gwen. I'll be over."
        "Mariam – anne?   spell it please
Oh, you're not sure how to spell it."
Or the receiver banged in my ear at a voice
        other than his.
I'm strangling the phone with its own cord.

FIELDS AWAY (CHAUTAUQUA)

Come lie with me
        in fragrant fields
        above the lake
Let other sweat at their pianos
        in the practice houses below
While we lie listening to cricket song
        our rhythm in heartbeats

FUCK AFFAIR

Mama   Mama   what foes fuck mean?
Jenny said she saw a brother and sister fuck
        under the grape arbor

Don't ever use that word again
        It displeases God
Why do you suppose you're in a private school
        so you won't hear bad words

Fuck whammy   whammy and juicy
        fuck fuck fuck   fuck
Fuck God   fuck God   fuckGod
        now I can't separate fuck from God
A sin   sin   God will make you say it out loud
        in Sunday school
        before he kills you dead
But it's stuck in my head like a big avocado pit
        fuck   fuck God   fuckGod
        fuckGod   fuckGod

OCTOBER SEA

Mine alone
            the sea
       October sea
No one near the surf
not all that cold
       the October sea
Mine   mine alone
       the shore tumbling waves
nobody here but just us sanderlings
far out a seagull sits the swells
       sand   sea   and me
       my private gym
crests for diving
foam bubbles tingling
swift sledding to shore
       my skin pummeled pink
sea mine   all mine
       October sea

RENDERINGS

Sounds   all the sounds
       by the lily pond mountain high
Pine boughs stirring their pine needles
       plopping droplets
Poplars hand-clapping their leaves
       gold fish plashing the waters
       take-off of bird wings
frogs squishing to lily pads
mutterings of breezes
       my dress in taffeta whisperings

STAIR CLIMB

Pictures climbed the stairs with me
     in my godmother's house at the edge of town
bedroom cold dark
     in the howling of dogs
lostness of train whistles across the hills.
     Sent upstairs from the party room, I pass
fierce warrior in the frame,
     dead dancing girl across his knees;
up to Hell's writhings
     chained sinners frozen   burning;
past fish-frozen ancestors
     on the way to the Angel of Death
      at the top of the stairs.
The pictures climb with me
     will always climb with me
      to the bedroom dark cold,
     snow sloughing off the roof.

ABOVE

Awakened this morning
     to a lake of clouds
     where the valley was
We're above them on our balcony
     above the clouds at last
valley gone to a lake of sky billows
     Soon the sun
eating its way into the valley bone

HORSEHEADS

Musty-dark hallway
opens to three horseheads
pictured on my great aunt's sitting-room wall
        black   brown   white
Neck to neck   nostrils flaring   veins starting
Thunder and lightning hourseheads
        in the town of Horseheads[5]
So scary I run out of the house

Horseheads again
        my child by the hands
horseheads far from Horseheads
thunderers on the wall of a motel room
I gold fast to my little daughter
        to keep us from running out the door

SAY SOMETHING

Suspended in winter silence
        on a windless day
I swim my mind past islands of sound
        cicadas' forte
        finches a tonal brook
wild horses thundering
scraps of melody
        my daughter's gone voice.

---

[5] Horseheads is a town in New York State, north of Elmira.

NAPOLEONIC GESTURE

No   it's not pomposity
        not pomposity
when Napoleon thrusts his hand
        inside his uniform
Fighting in all climates
        hand blue with cold
he is after something more than power

SUPPOSED TO BE ASLEEP

Conch shell to my ear
        from a long-ago shelf of home
snow falling from the roof
coal settling in the cellar
        branches tapping the window pane
voices from the kitchen
    sounding up through the register
party sounds from the living-room
      when I'm supposed to be asleep
Papa night-winding the clocks
winding me safe from lower hall
    to the landing on the stairs
to the clock in the upper hall

I put the conch shell back on the shelf
let a thicket of years spring up between

MARRIED

Married a blacksmith
      about the last of his kind
his anvil rings the mountains 'round
his arms ring me 'round
      Stands tall as the cedars
      bends iron to his will
eyes blue   blue peace
The very sparks are sparks from his forge
My wedding bells the winging of his anvil
      He smells of the forge   of wild grass
Married my blacksmith of the mountains
      married the mountains

WHATEVER'S UP THERE

Hill above our house
      Who lives there?
Why do I curl in from finding out?
      Dogs bark in the night on that hill.
I hear them in my bed at night.

If I can listen to a train whistling
      on past our village
If I can climb the dark stairs
      past the picture of death's angel
      holding a child in his arms
Why can't I climb
      can't I climb the hill
      to whatever's beyond?

STENCH

Drunk in the doorway
        drunken bum   garbage
bare feet   filthy
        (bums' shoes get stolen)
dirt-caked arms   grease-grimed nails
        urine spilling out on the sidewalk —
I hold my breath against the stench —
        loathsome creature —
but I am in the filth of hurrying past

ACTION FIGURES

Doll men
        cute as kittens
my little boy places the doll men
        in battle formation
weapons   tiny deadlies
        lasers   death rays   fire bombs
doll men
        killed and killing
        in their silvery space suits.
To some god on a blue-sky mound,
        are we warring grown-ups
doll men, too
        cute as kittens?

HOUSEWORK

Why in the chaos of my anger
Why in the sleepless
Why do I leap on the back of housework
      attack wayward closets
      clean out the desk drawers
      polish the copper
was mirrors looking beyond myself
      towards clarity?
I wax floors
      get down on my knees to stubborn spots
wrap myself in the scent of lemon oil
send my dust out to the cosmos
      Housework is sweating good
      draws my shallow breath
      down to the diaphragm
as I   woman
      create space fields in clutter

QUANTUM ASHES

My young daughter's ashes
      greyed with the sea winds
beyond the shore
      where I collected seashells
      and she collected glass
      azure glass   amber   green
        sea sculpted
Would the sea winds   sea waves
      could form ashes too on the quantum foam
      to the daughter of our sea walks

STITCH HOLES

Some have the dignity
     of being hit by a train
       a car at least —
I was attacked by a baby carriage
     something sharp
such as a baby aiming a knife —
my calf split to blood spurts
     about raw flesh chunks.

Staring up at the ceiling light
     I was stitched fourteen times.
Daughter dear, you knew how to soothe
with me crying out *My leg   My leg*
     I'll never be worth a second glance.
When we sunned at the shore
bemoaning the disfigurement
     of what was supposed to be
       my best feature,
you said   *A truly neat job —*
     they look like little embroidery holes
and we laughed

Ashes on the wind
daughter without voice to comfort me
     What would you be saying
to make me feel better over your going?

EXTRA

Moon's something extra
      something extra in the sky
fat gold watch   centennial medal
      left-over goddess
bulging our earth   our waters
      bulging us.
Moon never grows our seeds
not comparable to solar energy
      mirror that does no mirroring
Moon's something extra
      something extra in the sky

APRIL IN MANHATTAN

Tired   the Park
s-o-o-o- tired
      first day of April
My Park   my Central Park
      withered   wizened
Trees too tired to let go their last leaves
      broken branches   rusted pipes
sewer smell from a ditch of putrid water
      shriveled grass
S-o-o-o tired   my Park
      first day of April

NEXT SPRING

Mourning doves last Spring
built a nest on the fire-escape across
      I feared for the mother
      and the litle one
but the window stayed barred
      nest safe

Next spring the mourning doves returned
     the mother sits the nest
     the father guards
they remember   they remember

ORPHANED FOUR

Flowers or birds   which?
four baby finches
     orphans   still in their down spears
perch on our fire-escape buckets

Despite trees laden with goodies
     a street of gardens
they beak at our moss roses
     stems   buds   start of seeds
Maybe I could scare off grownups
     but not starved orphans
     still in their down spears

MINDING MY S's

S paths
       some man of the mountain
laid out the paths in S's
       sibilant snakes

Knowing nothing of his S stratagems
       I climbed to lost
finding neither the duck pond
       nor the stump carved to a throne chair
       nor eagle rock
       nor the ice caves
Clearing after clearing after clearing
       broken by pieces of S's
dark   darker   darkest
       from before Con Ed
S paths black between precipice and ditch

Lost   black lost
scratched by brambles   gouged by branches
caught by the hair like Absalom
       falling back to animal on all fours
expiring in a thicket of S's-s-s-s-s

Man of the mountain
       What next?   Treble clefs?

COMING OF

Color   color
I doused my paintings with color
into the very pores of the canvas
            splashed color   slashed color
No canvas large enough for my multi-hues
Took to spreading canvas on the floor
            painting with my feet

Then one rain-torrenting day
            I came of painting age
by being drawn to form
            color but a part
seeing cones cubes cylinders pyramids spheres
oil drums   three mile island towers
            tall trunks of trees
            curving paths   cliff verticals
Earth formed and forming
moons and apples   and so I grow
            paint grow

SUPPOSE

Suppose after years of bringing my daughter to detox
winding up by mistake in the Bellevue morgue
Don't you know where you are, the guard said
    over the Christmas tree on his desk
        you're in the morgue.
Suppose she is in heaven's detox
        handful of ashes   nothing to detox
still if we are made up of molecules
she could re-arrange them
her Jackie could re-arrange his
    for a walk down Barrow Street
he in his scuffie cap   she in her floppy denims
    she could be walking beside me and her little son,
with us yet flying the cosmos
    daughter of the wheat-gold hair

GRAVEN

Graven image
            Thou   shalt not
    no golden calves   no Baals
In the sands this late afternoon
        I want the sight of my dead daughter
            so much
        I pick up a sharp piece of clam shell
        and incise her face
ghostly as the rubbings of stone angels
        side-sweep of maybe hair
        like funereal Grecian folds
        eye-holes   nose-holes
lips I work into something of a smile
        In nowise my daughter
graven image here on the shore

MONARCHY

Tarnished pigeons of city streets
      I am above you
      above the rare ones coddled on roofs
        the pure whites   special browns
      even the ring necks
Above all of you
      Note my jewel shower
I am crowned[6]

SCARLET GLOSS

Glossy ibises flying our northern marshes
glossy ibises with their down-curved beaks
      hangovers from the Nile
black in flight   green iridescent alighting
      in the sun

Scarlet ibises down Trinidad way
your postcard pictures them scarlet in flight
      scarlet sparks against the blue
Trinidad   here I come

---

[6] The poem may refer to the white-crowned pigeon (*Patagioenas leucocephala*).

MY RIVER

River   my river
           out-tiding the Danube
           the Rhine   the Guadalquivir,
My river   the river I am:
As the Hudson finds its source
           in Lake Tear of the Clouds,
I find my source in the Hudson of my growing

THE *INTREPID*

Still great grey with us
an aircraft carrier so vast
      it can gulp the Hudson to a mud flat

Visiting the *Intrepid* I can say with the Bible
      my bowels are moved
The Stars and Stripes envelop me
      yet it's a blow to the stomach
      all those men alone in the crowding
youngsters from furrows   from elm-arched streets
      from study lamps
to be drowned or maimed or murdered
      Vast *Intrepid*
      pain spiked into its steel
Intrepid a winner
      on the bodies of our boys

CAN'T LET GO

Everywhere about the skyscraper city
        apartment above apartment above apartment
                windows above windows
                        rooftops
We have onto the cliff's edge
                of Christmas
long after dried-up trees are tossed out
                in their bits of tinsel
Santa still rides the rooftops on his sleigh
                Christmas wreaths   circle
                doors and windows
gift bows decorate lapels
                a crèche on the mantel
                shines the star of Bethlehem

WIND WHEN

Wind
        when it changes
May it scream up no hurricane
        wreck no ships
        nor blow me off course
Wind when
        may it only shift
        the waters of the fountain
                my way
cooling my face
        changing my hair
                to diamonds

WARUM

Where
	Warum	Why
Schumann asks in notes of music:
	Where are the birds sleeping?
	Where is the wind when it goes?
	Where are the mayflies of a summer's night?
		Where are you?

AFFAIR

Rain pearling leaves
Sweet sting in the face
	nectar on the lips
Rain tones many as droplets
	dripping from street awnings
	patterning bushes
thudding earth
purring into gutters
beating a tattoo on rooftops
	gurgling down rain pipes
	slithering along skyscrapers
I'm having a love affair with rain
	city rain

CRACK OUR CODE

FBI   bug our phone
Crack our code
We're plotting
How to crash small mags
Have you heard of *The Great Speckled Bird?*
The what?
The Great Speckled Bird.
How about *The Little Word Machine?*
Never heard of it.
Nausea sent me a rubber snake
rejection.
Divine Toad Sweat sent my manuscript back
torn to confetti bits.
There's always *Pig Iron* and *Dogsoldier.*
Look Quick — no no —
it's the name of a mag.
Don't overlook *Empty Boat*
nor *Jam Today.*
Over at *Laundering Room Review*
they called me "Dear Submitter,"
and explained my manuscript was lost
behind a radiator for two years.
Some dog at *Poets Yeggs and Thirsties*
chewed up my works.
Scrotum can't see me for dust.
An acceptance by *Nitty Gritty* made my day.
What about *Strange Faeces?* I hear it's folded.
So has *Sunday Clothes and Sandwiches.*
Come on   crack our code.

GO WITH

Fun sometimes
fun to let the weather be boss
        to get caught in the rain
        the cool crystal rain
taste rain on the tongue.
        Snow the same
lift your face to the snow
        taste the sparklets
like Turner   lash yourself to the mast
        of a ship in the storm.
Wind   go with it
        let it race you along
        have its will of your wilding hair.

THEN THERE'S

Balloons   confetti   convention hubbub
Life's a breeze   a breeze
        except for power failures   strikes   murders
        blood in the streets   drug chaos
but then there's the budding   leafing   flowering
        cats at windows
sky of stars

SHAPED

A pine cone   a feather   a piece of green glass
        a trinity shapes me
            to sand   sky   and sea

SNOWY

Snowy owl
            bit of baked sunlight
            high asleep in the birch
white birch in green quivers
            an owl or a tree climbing to owl sun
I Indian-step around the tree
            eyes shading upward
an owl of a tree
or a birch of an owl

BY THE COOLING TOWERS

Little brown church in the wildwood
Little brown church in the dell

Fieldstone church of Three Mile Island
        by the cooling towers of Babylon.
The Reverend rings the bells beside
the radioactive waters of the Susquehanna
        oaken pews empty of all but two worshipers
        the others on the refugee road.
The organist has fled with her music
only sound the crack   crack   crack
        crack of doom reactors

Little church   little fieldstone church
        by the cooling towers.

STEP OUT

Moon's a spoonful
        Beware the Ides
castoria moon
        Moon's Libya
        packed with terrorists
Mine the moon for gold
Look for the man in the
        only a swollen Buddha
        Gulf of Sidra
Khadafi on a tractor
posturing above the golden grain
        Puppy Khadafi
        blood on the moon
red flag by way of Libya
        Step out of the moon
            Plant a flag
Moon up there negotiable
        no longer for lovers

APNEA

Startling up out of the cavern of sleep
        science says   it means
        I stopped breathing for an instant
Nightmare   deathmare

Sleep angel   don't let me stop
        stop breathing in the night

THE SAPPHIRE, THE DOLPHINS, AND THE GOLDEN WATCH

Three remains of sun queen glory
three in the terrace house on sunset hill
Three in my lowlands marriage
    Star sapphire   gold watch and chain
        pair of dolphin candlesticks
Star sapphire found on the finger
        of my drowned brother
My husband set his heart on wearing the star
        brook-clear eyes pleading
lost it off in a washroom —
deeper than he knew he wanted to lose the ring
        of my god brother

Priceless the dolphin candlesticks as a pair
        in nereid green
            museum piece
until he forced a candle into the fluted top
        and cracked the glass
            on sub-purposes?
cracking the elegant past
where I live now and then

Gold watch of my father's father's father
        My husband wore it on splendid occasions
        Would let only my father's watch
        tell time for him in his hospital room
Of course it was —
                    did he want it to be? —
                        stolen.

LISTEN

Listen to
       listen to the
mocking bird
       Just a song up North
until migrant mocking birds
       began to linger
now we live the listen
       listen to the mocking bird
and I discover his name is a put-down
       by jealous humans
maybe he mimics a bit
       mostly he originates
his selections infinite
       cher cher cher
       turkey   turkey
       tovaco   vaco   vaco
       mutterings   mumblings
Pretty bird   pretty bird
he may have picked up
unless some bird picked it up from him
       whistlings   flutings
       legato   staccato   pizzicato
Listen   live-listen
       live-listen
to the mocking unmocking bird

DRUID ANGUISH

Druid that I am
I live in God trees
        Wherever I am
I suffer when forests burn to death
attacked by arsonists   careless campers
        lightning.
A continent away
        I smell the smoke of their burning
        the eating away of flames.
Back when trees were worshipped
        anyone who dared harm a tree
had to unwind his intestines around the trunk
        until he fell dead.
Trees give of their shade
        absorb carbon dioxide   release oxygen.
Long time growing   a great tree
        putting forth leaves   flowerings
        taking storm winds —
and I am the tree's Druid.

MUST KNOW

What poured you in this time
        Tell me   I must know
Nothing   nothing at all
        in drunken slur
Has to be something
        an infinity of something
Tell me   I must know
        What poured you
            poured you in
Go find out at Alanon
            at Alanon
Your child is crying —
        Don't you hear your child crying?
You are alone in primal seas
        pushing me back into land alone.
You have forgotten how to walk
        nor can you swim.
Your speech slurs back to save days.
What poured you in
        bulldozed fields
office towers taller than church steeples
        your sinuses
the plumber not showing up
        the burned pie-crust
dinosaurs into the dusty sunset.
Must know   must know under the blank blue sky
        I will sift through cosmic dust
            examine meteorites
            strange sea waters
        back to what poured you in

WHAT I PAID

My $5.95   I want my $5.95 back
What I paid to be inside the C.I.A.
            jacketed as an explosive best-seller
            first uncensored exposé
            by a former deep cover agent
giant hole torn in the mask
            time bomb

Contents   FI concerned with collection operations
            PP staff with action operations
            CI with protection of FI and PP
Is that a fact?
            DDP responsible for all activities of the CS
Really?
            Explosive compounds can be molded
            to resemble bread   lamps   dolls   or stones
Time bomb stuff for sure
            Records Integration Division
            is to the Clandestine Services
            what OCR is to the DDL
But of course
            Training sessions with foreigners
            not supposed to know they are in the U.S.
            called black trainees restricted
            to areas away from JOT
Give me back my $5.95   I want my $5.95
plus five hundred and ninety-five for pain and suffering

MEMORIAL DAY, DEATH DAY

So beau   so beau
    S-o-o-o beau-ti-ful
I cried joy tears

Memorial Day   Death Day
    crystal tears over balloon columns
            two and two
blue columns   red columns
        white
two and two and two and two
        rhythming the breezes
merged to our flag   our glorious flag
exultant tears on Memorial Day   Death Day

Persian Gulf in oil ooze
    gurgling for more cars   more cars
in exchange for death
    more death   more death
Balloon columns released into upper space
    flocks and flocks of death birds
turning my crystal tears red.

PET STORE MANAGER

Pet manager   Please
        the tiny gray mouse in the window
Please take him out of the lizard's cage
        I know the laws of nature
But please don't let that creature
swallow a mouse so exquisite
        from his curl-paper ears
            to his minute feet
Please   I know the lizard must eat
        but not that confection
All right   I'll take the mouse out
        Crickets tomorrow
we'll be getting crickets tomorrow

LADIES' ROOM

Who of a summer-sunny morning
walks her neighbors' dogs along Park paths
        a frolicsome living
Who ties them to a fence
        and runs into the ladies' room
flower print flying
yellow daisy braids in Rapunzel swing

Meets her killer in the stenching dark
        her rape   her death

Who dies walking her neighbors' dogs
        of a summer-sunny morning?

STAR WHERE

Star   Star Faithful
If her name were not Star
        Star Faithful
would we care how she fucked up her green years
        back in Mayor Walker's heidee ho?
Star's inconsequential life
politicians   lovers   on boat bashes
        up and down the East Coast
insatiable sea vomited her to shore
        tarred body bruised by flotsam
                probable murder
                case still not closed
entry in her diary after a motel night:
        horror   *HORROR*   *HORROR*
Star   Star Faithful
        case never closed

APRIL KILL

Hospital windows look out on
        waltzing leaves   the Vienna Woods
        in mid-April flowering.
Four nurses' aides are busy killing.
They are holding the noses of patients
and in the gasping for air
        pour water into their lungs
Why?   we ask   why?
        the Danube is no River Styx.
A killer answers: "The ones who got on our nerves
were dispatched directly to a free bed with the good Lord."

Not in Vienna   should never happen in Vienna
        hear the Danube dancing blue lights

JEANS AWAY

Bottoms   bottoms
          Jean bottoms up
               ads up   up up up
splitting tight
          sign of the lion   stallion
               Gloria Vanderbilt
          from shirt sleeves to bottoms
               in three generations
ass men   tit men
          ass man's day
poster bottoms   dozens at a see
          every hue but brown
twitching to bottom music   toilet rock
          chit receptacles
          in farting back-thrust

OIL-SLICK SPLENDOR

Peacocks spread their iridescent tails
    along the avenues
peacocks once trees
    until liquefied to oil
    for cars to come

Rain now brings forth the peacocks
    asphalt peacocks
    along the avenues

IMMORTALITY OF SORTS

Grade B movie script
                    if I ever heard:
Child prodigy   mouse pretty
grows up to be a violinist
                    with the Metropolitan Opera.
This opera house a Minos-maze
                    except to the employees.
The girl leaves the orchestra pit at intermission
for the dressing-room of a male dancer,
to suggest her husband design stage sets
                    for the dancer's German troupe.
Never returns to her violin.
They find her nude body bound hand-and-foot,
stuffed down a ventilator shaft,
                    skull fractured
                    from being pushed off the roof,
man-stains only on a nearby napkin.

Whodunit? Suspect in a cast of thousands.
                    How is that for a scenario?
Incredible trash.
                    That happened.

Might as well murder edelweiss!
She gave a concert at eleven,
                    in a demure dress,
practiced aching long in her dreams of concert stage.
No one noticed her at the music-stand
                    in the orchestra pit.
Murdered she is in the minds of millions,
                    in the hearts of many.
Murdered she lives forever,
                    her violin on an empty chair.

GLASSES TO THE WORLD

Take off your glasses
      your thick-rimmed glasses

But it would put me in a blur

Come on   take them off
      I've never seen your naked face

What's to see?

With the taking-off of his glasses
      I am almost blinded
      His are the eyes of a seer
      bluing into upper spaces

Into his glasses again
      back back nine-to-five

Already I'm missing you

ANYTHING BUT JELL-O

Jell-o jewels
        Dear vegetarian
How could you black them
        With word maggots
Saying for my sake   *any dessert*
        But Jell-o
As if it were a blood sac
        About to burst
Jell-o is not the innocent it seems
        It is made of the boiled bones
          Of slaughtered animals
So startled I drop the glass bowl
        Spilling the Jell-o
          To the bloody intestines
        Of a squirrel
          Struck by some don't-care car

ON THE GREEN

Balloons popping
while the soufflés fall
          at the Tavern
          the Tavern on the Green
Green with Mayors since its founding
          in Central Park

Balloons popping   pop pop popping
     to celebrate birthdays
          at the Tavern on the Green
food should turn us gourmet
          at this history place
but this squab
          pretty on the china
          tough in the teeth
Green grows the garden
wilted lie the vegetables
          on our plate
My friend's salmon has a tomato in its mouth
          a lemon in its eye socket

Pop pop   pop pop pop
I'd like to pop the chef in the eye
          balloons popping   soufflés falling
at the Tavern
          The Tavern on the Green

TROUBLESOME BALUSTRADES

Stairs of the mountain inn
    stairs from the 1890s
I hear changeable silks and crinolines
    on carpeting broad and deep
The balustrades carved of chestnut wood
all those flowering chestnuts killed
    by a plague of insects
The stairs   the great old mantelpiece
    epitaph of the chestnut trees

Wish I hadn't encountered the houseboy
    dusting the intricacies
    of the balustrades
Wish I hadn't asked
    What wood is this?
troubling me down from Queen
    to tired housewife.

SO I SCULPTED

My sculpture is in world museums
Stands stone wonderful
    among private and public greenery.
Few incomes can touch my least works.
Little girl playing in the park
        had one beat doll,
so I carved her a doll out of wood
from a fallen branch of the liquid amber tree.
    Returned to the park next day,
    I found her playing with the done-in doll.
Mine, she had thrown into the bushes.
    I picked my doll up tenderly.
You can see her any day
    at the Modern Museum.

THAT I AM

Fur birds   flying
                feathered lions priding
Creator *am that I am*
                cerise skies   purple suns
the ocean marigold
                petaled horses   leather flowers
cats all sparks
                rain ultramarine
rainbow snow
                people   green-leafed people
                flowering sometimes
bees making sapphires
                stones feather pillowing
pigs   the dawn clouds
                kitchen fields of sweet clover
that I am

DEPRIVED

Deprived means never having explored
    your mother's button box
fingering crystal buttons
    little brown buttons
buttons of silver and gold
    amber buttons   brass buttons
    pebbly buttons
sometimes a jewel   a belt buckle
    a brooch
Wonders all in the button box

EARS IGNORE

Ears
        I never noticed unless they flapped
        or stuck straight out
then along came Van Gogh's cut off
        Spock's pointeds
and I began to focus on ears.
Even the usual ears rather grotesque distractions
        from the face,
weirdly convoluted   rubbled like scars.
Better obliterated, these excesses known as ears.

Females   males too
        try to right such abuses with earrings.
Kids wiggle them into performances
        ears crawly as waterbugs
crudely sculpted gum wads
    What's to be done about ears?

TIME

Mountain mists when the last of Winter
holds stiff hands with the new Spring
        Peering through the mist slantings
I see circlings in the pond
        from creatures squirming up out of the ooze
        as our kind once did
see lily pads in search of lilies
hear the upper partials
        of the falling mist

PICTURE-POST-CARD CITY

Spikes in Liberty's crown
        draperies by the ton
I've been up in her window eyes.
        Empire State Building
        lighted red   lighted white   lighted blue
I've been up there.
        World Trade Center
I may not have mountain-climbed the outer walls
but I've been up inside the glass.

I live in a picture-post-card city
    my little boy a picture-book child.
    May not be Equity
    but I'm an actress off-off Broadway.
Had one two-year run
not to be said of most Broadway plays
    twenty-one performances   eight months   three.

I've been on TV
people recognize me on the street next day
    request my autograph
no mob scenes   no grabbing for a button or a buckle
    picture in the *Post*   the *Village Voice*
I've modeled   been painted
    my telephone keeps ringing.

A bit fabulous but not famous
    small apple in the big
I've been interviewed yet I need no dark glasses
    don't expect to be asked for my memoirs
no theater is likely to be named for me
    still I wear a spiked crown   climb mountains
live   something of a picture postcard life.

SURE

Coney   sure it's of the mind
        the yucked-up Gowanus Canal
        garbag'd streets
        smelly alleys
        rotting buildings
Springtime Coney
        glitter dust over all
grass asserts itself up through
        cracks in concrete
wild flowers alongside the fun tracks
        and the sea
unswimmable in its harbor pollution
        but horizoning in seeming purity.
Without a thought for Coney
        Spring hasn't happened.

Coney mind sure
Coney of the thrill rides
        that terrored me
Coney of the child I was
        big brother who was
        sure-legged through the revolving barrel
marveling   I took the safe route into Steeplechase

Coney on the mind of my little boy
To Coney   to Coney   my now in him
sees through a haze of cotton candy
        the bubbles of soft drinks
Merry-go-round not exciting enough
        for his nine years
The wonder wheel   will it be too tame
Nathan's   the Queen of England came to visit
        I inform him between bites of hot dog
Barkers in losing competition to the high tech noise
I seem to hear a street car from before
gleaming track bites through asphalt
        where the street car curved back to Brooklyn

The piano player in red suspenders
        and battered straw hat
        still there for me to shoot
My boy hurries me on to the video games

Salt of the sea past cooking grease
We climb rocks slippery with algae
        lean down into the barnacles
        laughing at splashes
His now   my now in him
        leaving him at the Cyclone
I ride the merry-go-round
        to my mind's Coney

MEANING WHAT

Passed away
            What do you mean
                            Passed away
            Stiff fish   bone dust
Away like milkweed feathers
            Dandelion clocks
Breezes across a pond
            Passed
Star point   toe point   pencil point
            Snow crystals
                        Away

WALKS ALL AROUND US

Boy at the almost-empty beach
          alone
about eight like our boy
milk chocolate skin   gray eyes —
          born we suppose to some Southern Isle
of palm trees handsome as the boy
          beneath his cap,
hibiscus over pink walls
coral roads to scuff along —
stares at us in wading
wades out in the chill April waters
     for more staring

When we run back to the sands
          he walks all around us
          staring unabashed
Uneasy the head that wears the white crown
          beneath ghosting seagulls
we tighten our hold on valuables
          The boy follows us back toward the boardwalk

When our little boy stops to fill a bottle
          with sand
the gray-eyed boy in his dark cap
          kneels to help
          saying not a word
As we cross the boardwalk by the wonder wheel
          Crying out   *Pablo   Pablo*
his Mother reaches out to him
          hugs her lost boy
darker-skinned brother and sisters group about him
          Pablo lowers his head
looking out from her ample breasts
          ashamed
as we fear-victims wave
          before boarding the wonder wheel.

INTERRUPTION

Nine
        lighting the nine candles
on my little boy's birthday cake
        I am nine
candles blowing out to sputter on again
        Invasion of my playroom
while I work up friction
to speed my fire truck along
    Papa walks in to tell me
my strong swimmer brother is dead   drowned dead
I keep right on racing my fire truck
    past the rude interruption

SHOULDN'T HAVE

Keep   throw away
            throw away   keep
Why aren't you here to help
            daughter mine
You shouldn't have stood me up for death
left me to decide what to do with your belongings
            everything with a memory
                hanging off it
            like a price tag

MORE FEELING THAN THOUGHT

I am cradling skeins of darkness
    in the fingers of my two hands
but who is holding the ball?
Could it be the lost one
    my mother   or my little daughter
    holding the globe?

Hair of sleepers
    tucked away in the dark
Sun hair   black shining
    brown of earth
Ropes   pigtails   curled
    frazzled   sleep-tossed
Hair on pillows of night

What day is this?
Iraq day?   Our day?
    Doomsday?
Day of tight buds waiting?
    Pollution day?
Crime day?   Lovers' day?
    Day to go forth

FOUND FACE

Subway people,
Miles of subway people,
Miles and miles of faceless faces,
    They sit across from you, beside you,
    Get up and go without your seeing.
Faceless beside me,
    He soon leaves the seat empty
    Except for his wallet
    Worn to the shine of old pilings.

Paolo Hernandez
In hopes of a returned wallet,
    His phone number in an address book,
Names of Rita   Conchita   Luana
His face is in his wallet,
    Fuzzy Fotomat pictures,
A young Hispanic making the most
    Of scraggle on his upper lip.
Picture on his identification card   lake clear
NYRA   that would be New York Racing Association,
    Bronx address   five feet one inch, eighty-seven pounds
    a good-luck condom,
Money   a five   a ten   a twenty   three ones
    Thirty-eight dollars

An immediate call brings his mother to the phone
    With God-bless-you's
Another voice. So you found my little brother's wallet.
Works morning six to eleven
    Grooming horses out at the race track,
    Wants to be a jockey.
He must have dozed off.

Sleepy Paolo beside me
In a dream of swift horses,
    His moving up along the rail to a win

Rush of rain when I go to meet Paolo in the Park,
Crouching under the tree house,
    I watch for him,
Motion him in where it's a little dryer.
Horses are stupid, he says,
    Counting out his money.
You have to be smart for them.
    If I lose a few pounds and meet the right people,
I'll be a jockey riding my horse down the stretch.
    Trying to light up in the wet,
    He offers me my reward,
        Here, try it. A puff of his joint.

CHRYSANTHEMUM

Lean actor   long of stem
hair white chrysanthemum
seeable clear across Washington Square
    white chrysanthemum
        before he died

Tall-stemmed
    white of hair
who walks by the fountain
    seeming to be
when he will never come again

OUT TO

Out to the Valley
Up to the Park

To be-ribbon the day
my mother would take me out to the Valley
    last stop on the bus
We would pack a picnic lunch
    and ride   just to ride
Getting off at the Valley
we would walk beyond the sidewalk
    into fields feathered with grasses
    picnic under an elm
wade a stream of slippery steppingstones
    banks orange with jewelweed
    hickory nuts to gather

Out to the Valley then
Up to the Park now
    with my little son
glacial rocks to climb
squirrels making much of their tails
    boat to row 'round a lake of willows
    lunch at the restaurant
        by the model boat lake
    watching the breezes fill toy sails

Up to the Park
Out to the Valley.

RED PEPPER LOVE

Red peppers
                sweeter than green
Market to market
                we searched for the red
red peppers and honey-crust meatloaf
                first dinner in your apartment
you played the harpsichord
                before it was stolen
and nobody was out to steal our moments
                that rain evening

Staying on
I shopped with you for red peppers
        sometimes we had to settle for green

Now you have a new harpsichord
        and red peppers I suppose
        honey-crust browning
while down my way
I shop for the sweeter red
        sometimes settle for the green

AT LEAST

Flies birds out of his fingertips
    so he can lens them for us laggards
bump on a branch   a whippoorwill
    yellow-billed cuckoo in the thicket
Quick   the knotweed   a mourning warbler

What's featured today?
Olive-sided flycatcher on that dead branch
    That's nothing after the cerulean
You should at least have a hooded —
    Grudgingly we lift lens to the olive-sided
Our Merlin lets us spoiled brats find our own feathers
when by ourselves we're fortunate if we can spot
so much as a ground-scratching towhee

OUT OF COMBAT

Take two
                two antlers
take them out of combat
                bring them together
two antlers in tip-touching arch
                and you have a shrine

PACEMAKER

Scanning the birds
Scanning lives
We stand a Park rock
    The white-haired one and I
Listening to the purple finches
I hear him tell of the greats he knew
    Paderewski   Caruso

Watching the pale warblers
    I see his mansion up the Hudson
He blooms stories beside me
Only because a pacemaker nudges his heart along
    With the perching of a flock
    Of cedar waxwings
He says, *My father had a music room*
As his voice almost leaves him
    I must run down to the boathouse
    To call an ambulance
When I only want to hear more of the music room

The ambulance drives off with all that he knows
    Please don't leave
    Don't let them drive you off
Before you tell me of your father's music room
Did it have a Pleyel   a Beckstein
Did Paderewski play?
    Caruso sing?
    Isadora dance?
Will you be back to our rock
To tell me of your father's music room?

TO THE TASTE

Lunch   luxury lunch
          with you
River bank in fireweed
          as we taste of the fruits
We build a collage of was and is and will be
          Lunch into the afternoon
no cubicled desk demands
          our watches make no noise
taste buds in the fresh of Spring
          from out the Muzak
a Schubert Impromptu of long-ago practice
          in the leaf-light of poplars
tablecloth of rose damask
          turquoise napkins
silver shine and irises in a vase
          You have the wit and I have the wisdom
          or you have the wisdom and I have the wit
through our words
          the celesta of ice in a water glass

NOT MUCH

Not much
          not much of a view
                              from my window
beyond fire-escapes and cornices
     cross on a green dome
Not much
          not much of a view

THE ONE SHOE

Day of the one shoe
    the Athena sandal by the sea
shoes well back from the surfing in
    I give myself to the winging waves.
Shaking off the salt-sea droplets
    I sun myself brown dry
    put on my clothes
      skirt a sail to the sea winds
    bend to my sandals —
      only one!
I footprint about eyeing everyone's bundle
    pitch toward every shoe shape
    explore the holes children dig
    look for a dog with one shoe in his teeth
    know every bit of driftwood surfed ashore
peer into trash cans buzzing with bees
    scrabble the boardwalk
      ask around.
Must hobble to the station
    avoiding broken glass
      board the trestle train.
Who would want one shoe,
    perhaps hating my red hair   my hammertoe
That backward child wandering the sand:
    would she toss my shoe to the surf
      with unaccountable delight?
Keep returning to the sea
    still searching   still wondering.
My missing shoe eclipses the sun.
    The sea is one big shoe.
Inflation overtides us,
    hurricanes devastate.
I am Athena
    and some paltry mortal
      has robbed me of my sandal.

REVOLUTIONARY ETUDE

Happened on a wooded path above the lake
A great virtuoso on his way up
        to his sunned white studio
Too shy to approach him
I was glad my mother and father
        gave me a gentle shove

What can I do for you   little girl?
Come along up to the studio and audition
Would it   would it be possible to study with you?
        Trouble is I fell down on my roller skates
and my right knee is too stiff to pedal —
        Why that would be like seeing you
        without make-up
which you are too first-flower to need.

At his concert grand resonant even to look at
        in the morning light
I sounded the keys to Chopin's *Revolutionary Etude*
Dry sticks without the glossing pedal

Knee healed   pedal glossing again
        I still couldn't keep up with the prodigies
Demoted to nothing more difficult
        than Beethoven's *Für Elise*

Just one of his pets I overheard a student whisper
        at Concert Class where I had yet to play
Just one of his pets
        along with *Für Elise*

MOON MILK

Moonstone
        mystic blue
      translucent silk
        my marriage ring
I gaze into its far blue white
        its adularescence
        on a space flight
        to the moon beyond you
Its night shine knows nothing
        of the sun of you.
I no longer want your everyday
        of typewriters   washing machines
        your blenders and hanging plants.
Darling, why didn't you play it safe
        with a diamond,
instead of losing me to the far blue light?

MIDDLE OF

In the middle of
                fiddle of
        middle fiddle
                of the night
Hours spinning counter clockwise
        plum tree and long cold sunlight
Letting go on the hammock
                cozy warm pee
Office desk nine till five
        philodendron greening in a pot
Patchwork   dropped stitch
        in the middle of the night
Worries
        in the middle of
                fiddle of
Neighbors impinging
        coughs   car starting up
                parrot screech
moon an ice-skating rink
        in the middle of the night fiddle
Brain a packed crate on the waves
        stage center   stageless
Are they stealing my bike below stairs?
        Milk bottles on the back porch
            frozen to sherbet before apartments
        milk bottles and lilies
Whatever became
        in the middle of
All those tubes up the nose
        at the VA hospital
All those leg stumps
        George   George
Chubby black-and-white kitten
        died at his saucer of cream

Burned toast in the middle of
        sphex moth paralyzes its victim
        eats him alive with the skill of a surgeon
I simply can't approve
        Marilyn Monroe is a fright at sleepless
Your beauty   get your beauty sleep
        typewriter tracks in the middle of
            fiddle of the night
Town of the midnight stab sun.

POEMS FROM COLUMBIA STREET
(LOWER EAST SIDE 1960s – 1978)

GREENWICH VILLAGE HISTORIC DISTRICT
BARROW ST
ONE WAY

HEART-SHAPED

Two thousand seven hundred dollars
   For a heart
  A heart-shaped bed
   To my order
Smoothed with satin sheets
   Strewn with pillows of satin
Lace-edged like a christening
   All in the pink
    Of a strawberry soda.
I want my heart-shaped bed
   As another might want a sailing ship
Yet another a field-stone house on a hill.

Heart-shaped
   Shape of my heart.
I have been in beds of loathing,
   Turned the quick trick
Worked the cribs
   Many Johns in line for a stinking mattress
    No time to remove their shoes
Been stooge for weird fantasies
   Bedded by ageing bachelors
Call girl sleeping between calls.
   Half dreaming half waking
I longed for my heart-shaped bed
  Dreaming into being my love,
   My heart's love.

ROMANCE OF THE HANDKERCHIEF

Let's play drop the handkerchief,
        Drop the handkerchief,
Drawn from the secret warmth
        Of her handbag.
A lady's handkerchief
        Lights up her fragrance,
        Flutters with her lashes,
Her fan   her come-on,
A favor   a fetish.
        Its lace suggests her lingerie.
Drop   drop   drop the handkerchief.
        Wait   don't bend your back.
Only a tissue   a dirty cleansing tissue
        She'll disclaim

FLAME DARK

Candles all burning
                        Café candles
        To flaming Farrucas
                        Siguiriyas
Death candles burning
        Hurricane candles
                        Love-supper candles
All burning to the center
        Dark center of the flame
                        Dark-pointing center
        Chilling as it warms
        Warming in the chill
Must I always see the dark
        Dark of each separate flame?

LISTEN TO THE NAMES

Listen to the names
      Music roll of names
Marilyn
      Rosalie
            Doreen
                 Veronica
Coffee-house where nobody stays
      Long enough to starch an apron
Names with the hanging-up of coats
      Mine's Eileen
        I'm Theresa
     I'm Roberta
        I'm Marge
        Elsa
Sea flower names
     Lorna
        Rianne
            Lilian
    Doris
      Gee Gee
Names many as sand sparklets

HENRY WARD

Henry Ward Beecher
     Came out of his Brooklyn Church
       This morning.
I ran to catch up with him
     As he went looking for his statue
       Moved far down the Plaza
     Rather out of the way.
And the ghost to his likeness muttered
I didn't care for my brother Tom's remark
    When he preached from my pulpit:
Those who came to worship Henry Ward
    Can leave;
Those who came to worship God
    Are welcome.
Seeing that I saw and heard him, he added:
If Richard Nixon had knocked on my door
    In the night like Abe Lincoln
      Seeking wisdom
There might never have been a Watergate.
Thanks for running to catch up with me.

SNOW ON THE PUMPKIN

   Snow on a farm pumpkin
     Usual as a wintering blue-jay,
      Expected as cord-wood.
Snow on the pumpkin of a cement city
     Snow like an Elizabethan ruff
About a pumpkin that survived Thanksgiving
     Without being a pie —
My morning window faces out
     To snow on a pumpkin
     In a January alley.

FIRSTS

Biking to a five-alarm fire
    Down by the docks
I wheel toward a yard in crocuses
    Gold   purple   and white
First crocuses of Spring
    In leaves of grass
Speed into smoke so choking black
    Cars turn on their headlights
Flames taller than the tallest flowers
    I wish I had stopped at the crocuses.

WATERMELON MOON

Watermelon moon
        As I phone about the broken icebox
Watermelon moon
        Red juicing to the lights
            Of the city plate
        While I phone emergency
Watermelon moon
        Paling as the repairman
Makes an estimate past my pocketbook
        Scraped shriveling into the night
Watermelon moon
        I appeal to you
Save my icebox
        Toward goodmorning melon

MY NAME

My name
      My name is
Three of us in the TV truth game,
Two lying   one telling the truth.
Standing under lights in the blaze of truth,
     Each tells the panel
My name is Martha Mayhew Evans,
     Which I am.
The emcee is reading my statement aloud.
     My husband and I live
In a Brazilian rain forest,
     Eating only the foods that grow wild
       Along the Amazon.

My name
     My name is
Brought up on the rules of health,
     Told what is good for me by my family,
      Good for me by my husband,
I hunger for fatty steaks and lamb chops,
     Everything high cholesterol,
Dream of continental chocolates
     Dropping like kumquats from the trees.
I would gather city lights as I gather
     Flowers in the rain forest,
Would rather have a boxed orchid
     From a steamy flower store.
Here I chatter as the monkeys chatter there,
     Letting someone else gather my food.
     My name
       My name is

POEM PORN

Shit   cunt
    And some say *Behold I have wrought a poem*
Shit and cunt and fuck fuck fuck
    Flourish of fellatio
Whisper of cunnilingus
    Cunning   cunning
        Lingus   Ah lingus
Cock cock cockado
    Cockadoodle   doodledo
Fuck fuck fuckado

HER OWN DANCE

Relax and enjoy it
    Dance it
The Park girl does
    Books under her arm
        On the way to class
A drunk with booming transistor
    Stumble dances
        Lunges back and forth
    Blocking her path
        Trying to grab.
Tensing at the cut-off
    She goes into her own dance
        In the joy of fountains
    Dances her own dance
Whirls around him on her dancing way

BINGO I'M NO BABY-SITTER

Bingo Gram I am
    Don't expect me to baby-sit
I saw the six of you
    Through all the diseases
Now it's your didie baby
    Upsa daisy turn.
I'm a swinging bingo single
    Off to the red and black squares
Nothing so wild free
    As a Bingo Gram
Shouting *Bingo*
    Bin-n-n-n-go-o

COMFY COZY

Rippling   rippling
    Miss the Watergate hearings
        TV's tenderizer
Such nice-looking young men
    Real haircuts   ties   starched collars
Miss their obsidian-slick diction
    That is correct
    That is correct
Any disturbance cool as wind-charms
    No need to listen good
They go on for hours
    It's like keeping company with a waterfall
As for reading all that garbage
    I don't have the patience.
Dean is for me
    And his Watergate wife
Sitting blond behind him
    With corsage and white earrings
        Like a *Vogue* blow-up.
So he took a little wedding money

Why if Dean were sitting in my living-room
    Planning to murder me
He would make it seem all right
    Senator whatever his name
Emcees the hearing like a Johnny Carson show
    All in the family
I like cozying up to government.
Never again, I fear,
Will there be anything like Watergate
    On TV.

HUSH LET ME

Dvorak's *Cello Concerto in B minor*
        Puts me together as it pulls me apart
Composed in America with a longing for his Bohemia
    Bohemian glass on the mantelpiece
        Above my grand
New World Symphony discovered a little past
    The honeymoon
    Loved it more than my marriage.
Music by humans
    A love beyond human
        Cresting my salt blood.
Next platter to drop
    The Brahms my love once gave me —
I reset to the Dvorak.
    Still on the noon street where we passed today
Something wouldn't let me speak   change expression
    To his lockjaw Hello
        Muttering of my name.
No Lot's wife, I didn't look back
    Nor, I suppose, did he
But I'm looking back   listening back   now
        Fragments of our together
Floating about in the Bohemian glass
    Hush   hush   let me listen

BIKING TOWARDS PIANO

Uptown they'll have it,
    The piano for me.
I bike the crumbling West Side Highway
    No longer fit for cars,
Highway mine
    Above the Hudson
As if the towered city gone to jackals.
Grands mine for the taking —

Dead   dead
        Dead   dead
The mutilated pianos
        I can afford.
Ghosting back along
        the carless overpass,
    I ride piano ruins.

OLIVE WOOD

One hour on the isle of Cyprus
    And I bought an olive-wood dog
Horror island now
    Invaded by the Turks
        Refugees huddling
In the shadow of funereal cypresses
    Blood island
I read in the *Times*
    See on TV
But know only the Cyprus
    Of the olive-wood dog

WILLIAM RANDOLPH'S YELLOW ROSE

Tall trees toppled to William Randolph's Empire
      Hearst uprooted trees to get at people roots
        In the dung mix of blood bursts
        Tear spatters   death threats
        Bombings   sex in a closet
        Urban guerilla unemployed
Yellow journalism   blood yellow

Grand-daughter Patricia   his yellow rose
      Making news when the papers are slumping
Name that fits headline space
      Patty wanted
      Patty raped
      Patty talks
      Patty weeps
Patricia is Svengali'd into headliner
      By her ghost grandfather
Marion Davies   the wild child   no such copy
      Patricia is his news mistress
The very flower of his journalism
      Sensational

How is it with ghost Hearst
      Having his grand-daughter a smash headliner
Perhaps turning yellow journalism to bile
      News drips out of her like a runny nose

If William Randolph had lived
    What kind of press for his grand-daughter?
Would he have created an actress upon world stage?

WOMEN IN FLOATS OF SILK

    Woman with a scarf,
Coming home from school
    I would follow a woman with a scarf,
Lean against a tree trunk
    And watch scarves float the women past,
        Wind-dance them down the street

    School books put by,
I married one,
    Married a woman with a scarf
        Of softer silk   more fold
    More wind-chased,
Rainbow seas   her scarf,
    Married her only to find
I wanted to wear,
    Am wearing,
        Her scarf.

HORSES GONE

Glad they're gone
        Glad sad
Horse or two around to remind
   Pulling junk carts   vegetable wagons
Victorian carriages through the Park
   No more horses over-raced
To the bursting of their hearts
   Beaten   doped   for a win
      Bloody with saddle sores
   Pulling loads too heavy
Work-horse is pained into the language
   Driven long hours   long years
Floundering up icy hills
   Shot after the breaking of an ankle
Roped out of the wild   hunted down by planes
     Broken to the bit
   Burned in stable fire
Glad they're gone
         Glad sad they're gone
   The horses

OPEN

Gone
    His door hangs open
Boy down the hall from me
    I was shy of him on the stairs
Looking into his room
   I see the same sad drapes
     Same scarred maple
   Same air shaft
    Same stale air
  As my room next door.
Tooth-paste cap on his wash basin
   Rusty razor blade
Milk container in his trash can
   Sandwich-wrapping   end of bread
    Last-supper like.
One wad of paper that missed
    the rusted can
I pick up   toss in   retrieve.

Alone, I unfold it to the late night.
Words in the empty-room night.
  A poem.
      Poem of alone.
I have one, too.

KEYS TWO

Typewriter keys
           Piano keys
  One by day
  One by night
Piano practice supples my fingers
  For fast typing of business bores
Subtleties of touch would only foul up the copy
  My piano fingers on typewriter keys
Are sail-ships lost on land.
   If I could only pull music
        Out of the typewriter!
Where are the rhythms   the rubatos
     Adagios   cadenzas?
Nights I sit at the piano
  Practicing scales and exercises
Going over difficult passages
     Over and over
  But never as boring as typewriter keys.
Typewriter keys
           Piano keys
When I am no longer a student of promise
  Playing my way to world concert stage
    I close the lid.
Through the fevered night of dreams
  I storm the piano keys:
Schumann's *Carnaval*,
    Beethoven's Emperor Concerto,
  Concertize until the alarm clock
Returns me to typewriter keys
  Rattle click   rattle click
    Rattle

NO LESS SWEET

No less sweet
            the ice cream
for the headlines
            babies butchered in black-and-white print
            by my chocolate chip dome
I spoon into the tongue-soother
            no less sweet
for the bloated bellies of starving refugees
            no less sweet
for the plane crash
            dead bodies strewing the wheat fields
No less sweet

BIRD OPAL

Flies
        I don't know where,
Schumann's *Prophet Bird,*
        Multi-hued bird of the mists.
On my stage I am winging the bird
    About the red-globed café,
Not the Philharmonic Hall I sweated toward
    In summer practice houses,
Running up to the field of barley
    Above the lake after a bad lesson.
Café piano balking   wheezing,
    The Prophet Bird no longer Schumann,
My bird of unknown prophecies.
    Practicing one Sunday afternoon,
People listening in the doorway,
    Close as I come to the encore crowd
At the foot of the Philharmonic stage.
    I am one of those little squid
Who died in lava eons ago
        To form the opal.

DUST SHAPES

People fragments of the subway train
         All centering me
Drabs of dust
     Taking momentary shape
They're beginning to swirl me out
      From my center.
Einstein-headed man with a cane:
      Will he make it before the door
        Closes on him?
Little black boys running away
      Away towards,
Mother brushing her plain child's hair
      To a sheen.
Rowdy howdy drunk shakes us loose
      From our center for a dust pinch.
What book is the boy reading?
      Something about the Renaissance.
Black woman's wig with a white part —
     Just what shade are black scalps?
A corn-row hairdo shows through earth-brown.
     Dust clouds form and re-form,
I with them
       Taking moment's shape

LIGHTED STATIONS

La lay   la la   lay
Let the timid have their buses
    We're undergrounders
front window up by the motorman
    on the river Styx yet super alive
dark tunnels   dark and long
        curves low

Coming on fast through the dark long
we near the palaces of the underground
        the lighted stations
Monarchs of the front window
we need fast footwork to protect
        our speeding turf
La lay   la la   lay

NIGHT BROW

Riffling the typewriter keys
Writing a tale of the city
        I pause
Stare into the crystal ball
        Of my high window
    Three spaces of seeing
City lights string in popcorn promise
        My mind in-staring
My own face in the window lake
    Brow set with horns
        Broken off to star fires
    All-seeing

THE JAMAICANS

Call a repairman in the night
	icebox emergency
and open the door
	to a husband and wife
who bring the Jamaican sun in with them,
	rhythming pale trees in their voices,
		lilt of the Caribbean.
He restores more than the refrigerator
	as the moon rises hibiscus
above the light across the river,
	sings at his work while we wives
		exchange recipes,
	compare islands.
Of course I can't offer them cold drinks
	beneath the splashing moon,
as from the heat of Jamaica
	the husband works toward preserving
the crystal cold of the North

CONES THROUGH

Bridge lights
			Reassuring spheres
Only tonight they are tiny ice-cream cones
			Is it a trick of mist?
Windows in need of washing?
			Or have I never observed till now
That bridge lights are ice-cream cones.
		I gaze through the cones
Looking for the shape of universe

THINGS

Oh the number of things
        The number of things:
Jewel-toned finches
        Singing in a shoe-repair shop,
Petunias in a hardware store window
        Petaling out over a saw,
Smell of creosote and spices down by the docks,
        Grass winning the cracks,
Nibblements by snowball fountains,
        Deep-scented corolla of the princess tree,
Asphalt pattern-paced in bottle tops,
Clam shell sidewalks.
        Number of things
Oh a number of things

WHAT BUT

What's fizzing?
        Messed-up air conditioner?
            Toilet bowl?
        Leak in the pipes,
            Shorted wires?
Elevators liquefying?
Shadow glass shattering?
        Why, it's rain
Rain down towers of glass and concrete
        To sidewalks of cement.
Would know rain right away
        In a wooden house
Down eaves into earth
        Swelling roots

WINDLESS

From my windless room
    I look up to a penthouse awning
        With word of the wind
A shuddering down   its length
        Scallops a flock of yellow birds.
Can't be all that wind out there
      When it is windless in here

AT PENCIL POINT

About to word the world
      I sit on my pencil,
        Snap it in two.
Point still perfect,
      Eraser no threat,
Blue shadow point on the white page
      I feel the jagged edges
Of words sharper for the break.

FROM OUT ITS GREY

Black despair
Reddish-brown   tension
Yellow   blah
Green   serene
My mood ring means to tell me
Whether I'm morose or ecstatic
Passionate or suicidal.
Instead from out its grey
My mood ring calls to me
Calls mountains away
Down from highest valleys
To plains and forests
Crystal closer it draws me to a river bank
I fall into the rainbow waters
Help   help   I'm drowning in my own ring
Black fish with rhythming tails
Are dreaming me down
To a cavern of moods
Spinning the multi hues to a white light
Ultimate mood holding me fast

INNER SEEING

My lid cups
fill with color swirls
asking to be interpreted
in the light of the third   the wisdom eye
globes floating like Christmas tree ornaments
Seurat dots
grottoes green and gold
motion paintings all
rapids   golden snowflakes
almosts   not quites
fore-image for my divining

MORE POEMS FROM MAGAZINES

PIECE OF THE ACTION

Man,
Did you ever want a piece of the action so much
That it bubbled outa ya like sweat?
     A plum purple Cadillac
With my initials in gold on the door,
     White chauffeur at the wheel,
Monogrammed silk shirts   velvet lounging jacket,
     A cabin cruiser and a sail-boat,
      Beach house on the dunes,
Japanese servants,
     An English valet,
   White nursemaid for my kids
No mind left over
     To worry about getting caught   sent up,
      Death sentence for cop killers,
    Right and wrong of it.
Ya know them think tanks?
     Well I'm in a want tank.
You won't find a well no deeper.
     I didn't mean for no old man
      To drop dead of fright.
I just wanted a wallet fat as his heart.
If that dame hadn't a screamed
     She'd be in good condition today.
I wouldn't hurt a kid —
   He just got in the way.
If the guy in the Park
     Had handed over his camera like he should
I wouldn't have stuck my knife into his gut.
     I never did like pulling out the blade,
      And wipin' it off,
Now I'm WANTED
     When all I wanted was a piece of the action

[Tear sheet from unknown magazine]

OFF-OFF BROADWAY'S ROUGH ON GOD

Boys   boys
        You're too rough on god.
Last night you broke his toe.
        We can't keep replacing him.

In our image
    Our own image
We created him

Those are merely your lines in the play.
    Where is your actor's control
Saturday matinee you fractured god's shoulder.
He has to go around with a silver pin,
    being careful.
You think god is safe
    Because we let him wear knee-pads —
Still, you managed to wrench his knee.
        It's embarrassing
    To tell people god is in the hospital
And announce a new god not on the program

Easy, boys, easy

    If you must method act
        Be more Biblical
    Have a little respect
In our image   yes
        But god

[Tear sheet – publication unknown]

SKYED ALWAYS

"Just at sunset I saw a dead seagull,
    Plump red in the surf." —
"Oh no, you couldn't have.
    A seagull never dies." —
"Drowned — dead.
    His wings sogged in oil,
Only the surf gave him motion,
    Rolling him in dead.
Nothing deader than a dead seagull."

Seagulls never die
    Nor even fade away.
A seagull is made of light,
    Bits of sky in take-off,
White crest of a wave.
    No gull ever falls.
The tides of the sea, the flight of the gull
    Are for always.
A seagull flies beyond seeing
    Into sky, into sun.
A seagull never dies.

[*The Midwest Quarterly*, Autumn 1961;
also included in *The Midwest Quarterly*
"100 Poems from 50 Years" issue, Summer 2009]

REGISTER HIS HANDS, HE'S A KILLER

Poison berries hang in green-grape clusters
    About the red-candled cave
        Called Café Cadiz.
Hands contorted by karate,
    The flamenco-playing owner,
Commits karate nightly on his guitar,
    Thrilling tourists who never heard flamenco
        Into ragged *palmas* and *pitos*,
    Cries of *el duende*,
This cold-fire hate from a Cape Codder
    Who claims a Spanish grandfather,
        Guitarist from Cadiz.

Flesh hanging grey-loose beneath poison berries,
    He looks past help of blood,
        Embalmed.
In his late thirties,
    His is a face so old it sloughed off expression
        Unmarked time ago,
A plaster face   expression lines left unsculpted,
        Sockets beneath night sun-glasses,
            Rats at dead eyes,
His incisors seem to fizz green,
        Poison ring of a male Borgia.

Waitresses and entertainers
        Fired   about to be,
    Quitting   about to,
Cluster beneath the poison berries,
    Blood the red-candled cave
        Spitting out his violence,
Weaving the causes like a burdock blanket
        For a rabid dog.
Grew up in reform schools,
        Escaped a mental ward,
        Never made the concert stage —

This café is all he has of Empire,
          Napoleon on Elba.
They paste the labels on his dark glasses:
          Paranoiac   Schizophrenic   Sadist,
Can kill at a whispered word,
          A perversion denied.

Police should be manning the shadows.
          Someone should commit him before he kills.
Instead they pick the poison berries,
          Squeeze out the juice.
A drunk he slammed against a car,
     Entertainer he knocked through the plate glass,
Waitress he struck down,
          Five stitches in her scalp,
Canny enough to hire missing kids
          In too much trouble with the police
          To bring charges.
Hates women,
          Hates men, too,
     But women worse.
If he would give in to what he really wants,
     And we don't mean waitress women,
He might not be so violent.

Café street knows him,
     Police know him,
We know him,
As if everyone sees time disintegration capsules
     Exploding the globe bit by bit,
       See it and let it happen.
     For this is tambourine street,
       Folk song murder song street,
     Billy the Kid, Lord Randall, Comancheros,
       Fierce flamenco street.
Fun to talk about the mad guitarist,

Karate-chop flamenco,
Whose hands should be registered as instruments of death.
    Feed what he is into a computer
        And it will come out murder.
He almost writes magic marker
        Across the washroom mirror,
Stop me   Stop me now   before I kill,
And we paint the words funny-face,
        And mimic his karate flamenco,
        His chop chop down skull,
Make a Mardi Gras of his killing to come.
His only quietude is to sit at the cash desk
        Reading murder books,
Sadist's delight
    To humiliate
            Which he does,
Torture
            Which he does,
Kill
            Which he will

We all know where our next murder is coming from,
        And stay in its way for the café fun of it.
We play ring round the rosy,
        Ring round the crazy man.
We didn't know about Pearl Harbor,
        But we know about this,
        And let it happen.
He will kill   and we will cluster
        To pick the poison berries
If we're not the ones he murders.

[From an unknown chapbook or broadsheet.]

<144>

SEA WAIT

Winters I touch toe to the sea
     For an aching moment of ice
The May day my toes stop aching
     I will inch into chill waters
     Linger into October
I am that true to a sea often cold to me
     I play his white heard
Love him like a dictator
Terrorizing the rest of the world
     Tender with me
Never concern myself with the fierce deep
     Sharks   stingrays   barracuda
They're the sea's big affairs
     Nor do I settle for a swimming pool
I'd rather wait for the summer white beard
Though he brings occasional unpleasantness
     Sting of jellyfish   scare of sharks
Hurricanes get caught in his beard
     And I must watch out for rip tides
But soon the sea will toss me white roses
     And I will let out my hair to the sea

[Tear sheet from unknown magazine.]

ALPHABETICAL INDEX OF TITLES

ABOUT THIS BOOK

The body type for this book is Aldine, designed by Hermann Zapf to complement his earlier typeface Palatino. Aldine is named after Aldus Manutius, the great Renaissance humanist printer and publisher, who based his font designs on letterforms from Roman stone carvings. Titles are set in variants of Franklin Gothic, one of the great classic display faces of the early 20th Century. When this face was designed by Morris Fuller Benton in 1902, the term "Gothic" was used to describe modern-looking sans-serif typefaces, quite contrary to today's conception of "Gothic." Although the face has had many competitors, and faded from view between the two World Wars, its use resurged in the 1940s. Its distinctive letterforms and legibility kept it in type catalogs through the phototypesetting era and well into the digital era. Since it was a "hot metal" font originally, it also blends well with the urban cityscape engravings chosen for the cover. American wood engraver John DePol (1913-2004) consented to have details from four of his engravings used as covers for this series. DePol grew up in Greenwich Village and drew locales around Emilie Glen's Barrow Street residence since his childhood. The illustrations inside the book are photos of Glen's Greenwich Village neighborhood and her house, taken in the Summer of 2016. Sites depicted include Barrow Street, Cherry Lane, the Jefferson Market Library, and Washington Square Park.

9 780922 558872